Praise for the Dating Goddess

The *Adventures in Delicious Dating After 40* series of books is based on the blog Adventures in Delicious Dating After 40 at www.DatingGoddess.com. Here are comments from readers.

- "Adventures in Delicious Dating After 40 is a wonderful composite of both the mechanics of post-40 online dating and what the practice of honoring one's self actually looks like. How marvelous your writing is to read. I spent about 2 hours reading and was riveted the whole time." —Maggie Hanna

- "At last, a dating writer who addresses requirements. You are SO right on! I'm thrilled to have found you!" —Rachel Sarah, author, *Single Mom Seeking*

- "Powerfully heartfelt and honest writing. You are inspiring." —Kare Anderson, Emmy Award winning writer

- "I just love your writing. It is very fresh and gives the reader something to think about." —Kelly Lantz, President & Manager, 55-Alive.com

- "Dating Goddess, you are like a, a, a, well, a goddess to me. You've helped guide me successfully through my re-entry into the dating world after 14 years. I'm an eager student and fast study, and do get myself into situations that others don't know how to deal with — such as 3 dates in one day — so thankfully you are there! You're the greatest, thanks for all you do for us!" —Jae G.

- "I find your point of view much more interesting than other dating writers. Thanks for always reminding me to enjoy dating life no matter what it throws at you." —Sandy

- "I love Adventures in Delicious Dating After 40. I really do like your honest and authentic voice — it's refreshing." —Wendy S.

- "Adventures in Delicious Dating After 40 is really fun to read. Thanks for sharing your thoughts and letting us divorced single women know that we are not alone. There's a lot here that I identify with, although I'm not as brave as you are about dating lots of guys. So far. Love your blog — the first blog I've ever read consistently." —Elizabeth

- "Thanks for a wonderful blog. You're doing a great job of saying what's in my mind. There's rarely a day I miss when it comes to checking in on your wisdom." —Paulette Ensign

Ironing Out Dating Wrinkles

Work Through Challenges Without Getting Steamed

by Dating Goddess™

Embracing Midlife Men: Insights Into Curious Behaviors

Second Edition

Cover design by Dave Innis, www.innisanimation.com

Book design by JustYourType.biz

Printed in the United States of America.

ISBN Print: 978-1-930039-36-0

eBook: 978-1-930039-14-8

How to order:

The *Adventures in Delicious Daing After 40* books may be ordered directly from www.DatingGoddess.com.

Quantity discounts are also available. Visit us online for updates and additional articles.

The Adventures in Delicious Dating After 40 books are dedicated to my ex-husband since he unexpectedly released me to explore the untethered life of a single woman. I then had the freedom for the experiences, lessons and insights shared in these pages.

Books by Dating Goddess

- *Date or Wait: Are You Ready for Mr. Great?*
- *Assessing Your Assets: Why You're A Great Catch*
- *In Search of King Charming: Who Do I Want to Share My Throne?*
- *Embracing Midlife Men: Insights Into Curious Behaviors*
- *Dipping Your Toe in the Dating Pool: Dive In Without Belly Flopping*
- *Winning at the Online Dating Game: Stack the Deck in Your Favor*
- *Check Him Out Before Going Out: Avoiding Dud Dates*
- *First-Rate First Dates: Increasing the Chances of a Second Date*
- *Real Deal or Faux Beau: Should You Keep Seeing Him?*
- *Multidating Responsibly: Play the Field Without Being A Player*
- *Moving On Gracefully: Break Up Without Heartache*
- *From Fear to Frolic: Get Naked Without Getting Embarrassed*
- *Ironing Out Dating Wrinkles: Work Through Challenges Without Getting Steamed*

Contents

Introduction

This book is designed for anyone who is interested in stories, advice, and lessons from the midlife dating front. If you are over 40 and haven't dated in a while — or even if you have — you'll learn ways to approach dating with zeal, optimism, and hope. Even if you've had more than your share of negative experiences, I'll share how to glean lessons from those adventures, rather than just declaring that "all men are jerks" or "men are just looking for sex."

While most of the perspective is from a woman to women, men's comments, experiences, and lessons have been integrated as appropriate.

This book began as daily entries into my blog, Adventures in Delicious Dating After 40, which has been featured in the *Wall Street Journal* as well as on radio and TV. I wrote about my epiphanies from my and my friends' dating life. The best postings were culled to make this and subsequent books.

This book focuses on better understanding midlife men's behaviors that may make you scratch your head wondering, "What could he possibly be thinking?" Men are wonderous creatures, so we need to understand them better and love them for who they are.

This book consists of three types of perspectives:

- ***Lessons:*** These are specific experiences I thought would be useful to you. A few lines from my experience illustrate the points.
- ***Insights:*** These usually start with an experience I've encountered, then the insights that experience spawned. It is usually comprised of around half story and half insight.
- ***Stories:*** These are examples of situations I've experienced — or was currently experiencing when I wrote that piece — that I thought would be entertaining. Or I thought the story would help you see what kind of things happen in the midlife dating world so you'd know what has happened to others.

Because these writings were real time, as they occured, they are often set in the present tense. But they are not chronological. So a reference to "my current beau" may now be many sweethearts ago. I hope this isn't confusing.

I'd love ot hear your stories and questions. Please email them to me at Goddess@DatingGoddess.com. They may make it into the blog or my next book!

Who is the Dating Goddess?

I am a middle-aged, white, professional woman. My husband of nearly 20 years left me in April 2003 when I was 47, 11 days shy of 48. After giving my heart time to heal from the surprise divorce sprung by the man I thought was my soulmate, I started dating 18 months later. Generally, I have had a great time meeting interesting men, some of whom became romantic beaus, some became treasured friends, and some I never heard from again.

I am not a well-preserved, gorgeous, marathon-running middle-aged women

In the beginning, I had dates with single male colleagues, but I quickly found Internet dating was the way to explore the most "inventory" and qualify men who I thought might be a good match.

I am not one of those well-preserved, gorgeous,

marathon-running middle-aged women. I have been told I am attractive, but I am overweight and not a gym rat. So while I am active, I do not match the description 90% of men's profiles say they want: slender, athletic, toned, fit. I have some wrinkles — what one sweet suitor mistakenly called dimples. I have what Bridget Jones called "wobbly bits," as most non-surgically enhanced middle-aged women do. My genes — and a lifetime addiction to chocolate — have made their mark. Yet I've met and dated some wonderful men, so even if you're not a lingerie model, you can find guys who will think you're attractive, perhaps even hot!

In my professional life, I am a bestselling author of workplace effectiveness books, professional speaker and management consultant. I've appeared on Oprah, 60 Minutes, and National Public Radio and in the *Wall Street Journa*l and USA *Today.*

This book is intended to not only be useful to others and cathartic for me, but is also the genesis of a new topic for fun, thought-provoking speeches. I'm calling myself a dating philosopher and giving date-a-vational speeches! Let me know if you know a group who would like an entertaining after-lunch speech on how lessons learned from dating have implications in business and personal relationships and well as life philosophies.

How did I come by the Dating Goddess moniker? After a few months of dating dozens of men — one week yielded 7 dates with 6 guys in 5 days — my friends dubbed me this name. I liked it, so it stuck.

I'm purposefully not sharing my picture as I don't want you to think either, "How did she get any dates at all?" or the opposite, "Of course she found it easy to get 112 men to ask her out." I am not hideous (usually) nor am I stunning (without professional hair, makeup and Photoshop!). Some men find me attractive, some don't.

I continue to search for my "one," but I have learned a lot along the way, and my single and not-single friends have loudly encouraged me to share my experiences and lessons in the hopes of helping others navigate the adventure of dating with more success. And to have a delicious time doing it!

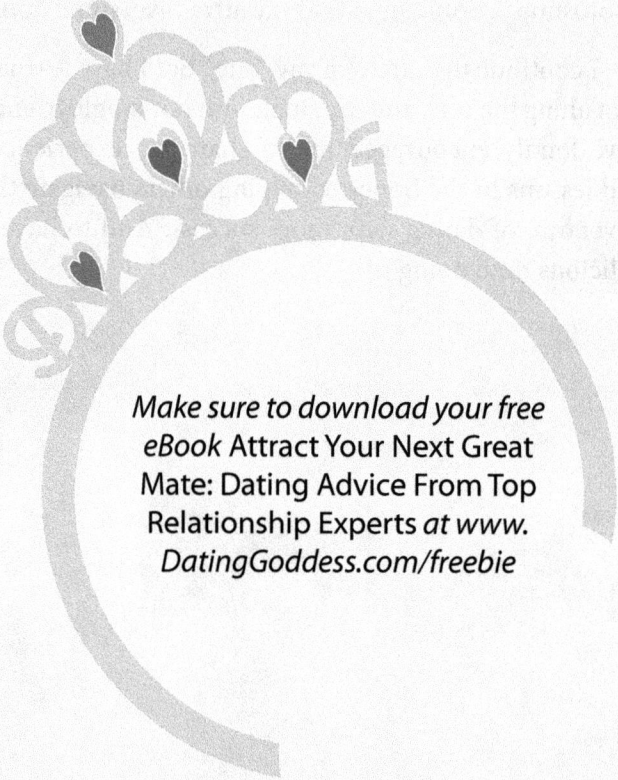

Make sure to download your free eBook Attract Your Next Great Mate: Dating Advice From Top Relationship Experts *at www. DatingGoddess.com/freebie*

Men are like shoes

I was hunting for date shoes in my favorite shoe store, DSW (Discount Shoe Warehouse). It is a cavernous store carrying thousands of varieties. One shoe per style and color sits atop a column of that style's variously sized boxed shoes. As I slowly cruised each long aisle scrutinizing each style, I felt like a too-lonely bachelorette prowling a singles bar searching for Mr. Right. Then it hit me — there were many similarities between dating and shoes!

- The pictures don't always match what's inside. At DSW, a picture of the shoe appears on the box front. However, sometimes the picture doesn't match the style or color inside. Often a man's online profile picture doesn't match his 3-D self. Or his picture is of him in a tux, when he is much more comfortable in jeans — a mismatch of picture and the true man.

- When shoe shopping I pass on 95% of the options. They just don't fit my taste, so no sense even trying them on. In dating, I pass on 95% of the men who the dating services say I match.

I just don't find most of the profiles alluring enough to give them a try.

- Finding a great pair of shoes takes time and diligence. You have to look at dozens — if not sometimes hundreds — of pairs to find one that you love. Which is the same with finding your life mate.

- Sometimes a pair of shoes can seem perfect until I try them on. Then they pinch or hurt and I can't stand to wear them. I return them to their box for someone else to try. Some men seem perfect on paper and/or over the phone, but within the first encounter, I can see it's not going to work. I return him to the dating pool for some other woman to try.

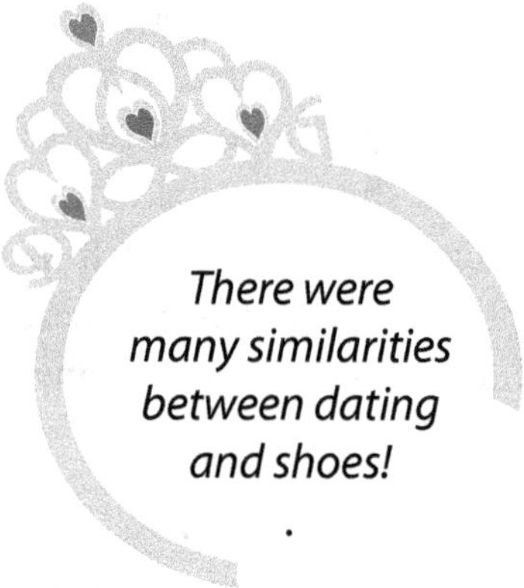
There were many similarities between dating and shoes!

- When I find a pair of shoes that initially fits well, I wear them around the store (or shoe department) while continuing my shopping. More times than not, they begin hurting within 10 minutes. But if I hadn't taken the time to test drive them thoroughly, I would have taken them home with only a 60-second trial. They would languish in my closet and I'd be unhappy I bought them. With men, if you don't give them a thorough trial period and jump to commitment too quickly, you may find you've made a bad choice. You'll be unhappy with yourself. You need to try out the relationship for a while before making a purchasing decision — I mean commitment!

- Some shoes make you feel frumpy and unattractive. While a man can't make you feel anything, some treat you in a way that you feel sexy around them, while others ignore you and you can end up feeling unattractive. Don't ever invest time and energy in shoes or a man with which you don't feel magnificent.

- Just as you need shoes for specific purposes, like hiking, running, dancing, golf, business, or formal wear, seek out different men for different events — one likes the opera while another loves country dancing; one cries with you at chick flicks and another accompanies you to a sporting event. So it can be useful to see several men for different outings.

- I'm really looking for a pair of shoes that are comfortable, versatile and appropriate for a variety of situations. Of course, I want a man who is all these things as well.

- When I find a pair of shoes that I love, I wear them often and treat them well. I polish them and keep them in good repair. When I find a man I love, I work to keep him happy and the relationship in top shape.

- Some shoes have good soles and some men have good souls. And there are some obnoxious heels.

So enjoy your shoe/man hunt!

Why men disappear when it gets serious

Gina Barreca authored, *Perfect Husbands (& Other Fairy Tales): Demystifying Marriage, Men and Romance.* Dr. Barreca is an academic who can make all that stuffy research come alive through her gift of humor and insightful writing.

This book tackles understanding the perception of marriage and the evolving roles of husbands and wives. She uncovers men and women's true feelings about commitment and marriage. And no surprise, many men are not thrilled with the concept of marriage! Even (especially?) married ones!

Her insights shed some light on why some men, even mature, sane, caring midlife men — can run the other way when it seems the dating relationship is getting too serious. One telling story was an exercise she had her college classes complete. She asked each student to anonymously and candidly write one word they associated with the word "husband." The only thing they added was their age and gender.

Granted, we could argue that their responses were skewed by their age — generally under 22. The majority of responses by the men were things like trapped, caught, p-whipped, while women's were nearly all positive: partner, companion, friend, lover, provider. Coupled with interviews of older men, both married and unmarried, she reveals that many men see marriage as something they are tricked into and they got the short end of the deal. After the first few years of the honeymoon stage, many men report they feel stuck.

While we can't declare this one book to be the reporting of a trend — especially since it was published in 1995 — we can better understand why men would feel like bailing when a dating relationship gets closer than he'd like. All is blissful when he can see his lady on his terms, when he wants and for how long. However, when talk shifts to long-term plans, moving in together, even marriage, some see their lifestyle switching in a way they didn't really consider before. After all, he likes his condo, his boys' night out, his ability to leave his underwear on the floor until someone is coming over. He can eat directly out of the can over the sink, use paper towels for napkins, and his shirt sleeve for a tissue. Who's to care?

Gina quotes Rita Rudner, "If you never want to see a man again, say 'I love you, I want to marry you. I want to have children' — he'll leave skid marks."

So what are you to do if you want a committed relationship, perhaps even marriage? My suggestion is to discuss the concept academically. Not "How do you feel about marriage?" but something like, "I read a book about how men and women feel differently about the words 'husband' and 'wife.' When you hear the word 'wife' what words come to mind? And 'husband'?" Play this with him and share your words — honestly. And see what comes out of his mouth. Don't argue or get upset. Allow him to say negative words without jumping on him. He may just be letting you in on the truth.

I remember on a first date that was going really well, I asked my date why he was now online dating when he'd been single for a few years. "My secretary signed me up. She said I needed to get laid." I said, "And why did you let her post your profile?" "Because she was right!" While I thoroughly enjoyed this man's company, it was soon apparent he only wanted one thing — and it wasn't to have a meaningful relationship!

People will tell you the truth if you ask gentle questions and don't argue or make them wrong for what they say. Just listen and see if what he says aligns with your values. And know that while some men can say the "right" things and act like they want commitment, they may still go poof when things get too serious for them. Of course, there are others who yearn for a long-term love and know all that this means. The trick is to separate the ones who don't really know they want to stay single from those who know they want to be coupled.

Chivalry isn't dead — but it seems to be hibernating

A few of my dates have had impeccable manners. Most weren't brought up in a house of privilege. Some were taught how to treat a woman by their mothers. However, if their mothers didn't teach them, at some point they decided it was important to learn and practice chivalry.

What do I mean? Holding doors, holding the chair and seating a woman at a restaurant, opening the car door, helping put on and take off her coat, walking on the outside of the sidewalk, making sure she orders first, walking together instead of ahead. These aren't big behaviors to learn and practice. However, I've noticed few men — even educated, successful, accomplished men — do any of them at all, or if they do, it's happenstance, not consistent.

Am I expecting too much? My women friends don't think so. Nor do those who practice chivalry regularly. I love it when a gay friend escorts me to important events when I'm in between beaus, as he is the epitome of chivalry.

So why don't more men practice chivalrous behaviors, even if they are not with a woman in whom they are interested? Holding a chair for a coworker or standing when a gal pal walks into a meeting is over the top. But opening doors for them isn't.

Sometimes women respond poorly to well-meaning chivalry

Are these difficult behaviors to learn? Hardly. Carolyn Millet holds classes on manners to 12-year-old boys and girls. She teaches the boys how to be chivalrous and the girls how to respond graciously.

I know sometimes women respond poorly to well-meaning chivalry. They confuse respectful manners with demeaning behaviors. I don't. In fact, I think chivalry indicates a man's respect for a woman.

So how do we awaken the manners hibernating in a man? Employ the "catch him doing something right" technique. Always thank him when he opens the door, helps with your coat, etc. If you want him to help with your coat and he hasn't in the past, gently hand him your coat as you're leaving. Unless he's really obtuse, he'll get it. Tell him "I love it when you do chivalrous things. It makes me feel cherished." Some get it. Others don't. Those who don't may find that when they do awaken these behaviors, they'll find mating season is over.

Do you reject someone for intermittent or non- existent chivalry? It's up to you to decide if this is a deal breaker or not.

Charm school for men?

Don't you wish there was a charm school for men? (I know men who would like to have one for women.) The challenge is the ones who really need it wouldn't register. If these were available for midlife daters, perhaps it should be co-ed and we should all be required to attend before saying we are interested in dating. It would certainly make dating for both genders so much easier.

In the *San Francisco Chronicle* article, "Charm school for men teaches the art of the pickup, or keeping the conversation ... going," writer Reyhan Harmanci discusses a charm school different than the one I'm envisioning. Yes, students get taught the art of conversation and how to keep the discussion 50/50, but it's all for the purpose of picking up women. It is easier to woo and charm a woman if you have poise, manners and conversational skills. Perhaps that's how to sell the concept to those who otherwise wouldn't invest the time and money.

I had three dates with an intelligent, funny, attentive man 13 years my junior. While we enjoyed each other's company, he drove me crazy by lacking some basic social skills. When he walked five paces in front of me, I had to tell him not to leave me in the dust. He interrupted me, didn't call when he said he would, didn't open doors, or other basic gentlemanly acts.

However, he had other positive personality traits, so I considered saying, "Let me show you how to get any woman to fall for you." If he agreed, I would tutor him in basic social skills and chivalrous acts that obviously his parents neglected. But he was gone before we could have that conversation.

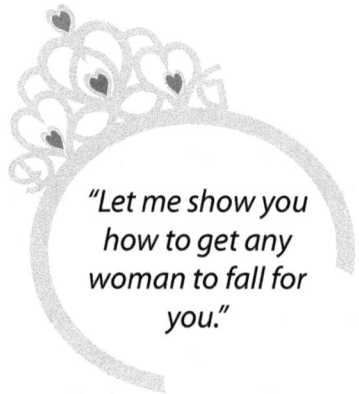

"Let me show you how to get any woman to fall for you."

Another man, 10 years younger, had also missed rudimentary training. He commonly went through doors ahead of me without holding them open. Since it seemed we were going to be seeing each other for a while, I wasn't willing to put up with his lack of manners without saying something. So I did.

Although these two examples are of younger men, there is no age limit for those needing a few reminders or hints. When a date does something charming, I comment on how I love it. I'd rather give positive reinforcement than negative, as most people can't easily handle being told they aren't doing something right. I feel the same way, but if a guy I'm seeing tells me gently and caringly that what I'm doing isn't working for him, then I can hear it. So I try to do that with my guys as well.

It really isn't that hard to be charming — and most women melt when being charmed. But if you aren't taught and aren't astute enough to pick it up yourself, you need to learn it from someone. And while some people take charming to a sleazy level, true charmers know the boundaries and don't overstep them. They are classy and you feel better having had a conversation with them.

Learning about male magnetism from ... rats

Perhaps you've lived this common scenario: You've dated a guy a few times. You hit it off and enjoy each other a lot. You feel great around him. He treats you well when you're together. However, he calls unpredictably, emails periodically, and you see him only sporadically. If you call him, it may take him days to get back to you. Yet you anxiously anticipate the next contact.

We can only guess what's going on with him. Is he game playing? Toying with you? Have another woman (or women) on the hook? Not that interested?

But then he calls or emails, and wants to see you — today, tonight, or now.

Since we don't really know what's up with him, let's look at what's happening with you. Many women get snared into this "hook, let out the line, then reel her in" behavior. Why do we fall for it?

B. F. Skinner explained it, thanks to experiments with pigeons and rats. He showed that animals (and by inference, people) are more likely to do what you want with intermittent reinforcement rather than consistent rewards. So for us dating midlife women, it means that we are more likely to be drawn in by a guy who gives us irregular reinforcement (infrequent calls, unpredictable emails, and spontaneous dates) than with a man who is consistent, regular and predictable.

I can hear you now: “Not me!” you say. “I like a man who calls me every day during lunch, has a standing Friday night date, and emails me first thing in the morning. Yep, I’m for Predictable Man, not Flake-o Guy.”

“I’m for Predictable Man, not Flake-o Guy.”

Well, good for you. You might be an anomaly if you’ve never felt yourself drawn to one of those intermittent-contact guys. Many women find something irresistible about a “bad boy” who comes and goes at his own whim, leaving you wondering when — and if — he’ll be back. But he’s so charming, attentive, exciting and smooth when you’re with him, you’re willing to put up with some uncertainty for that hit of his musty cologne, those goose-bump inducing kisses, and his adorable crooked smile as he sweeps you off your feet.

So what to do if you become aware that you’re entranced by an Intermittent Guy? If you like the excitement of spontaneity and unpredictability and like to be non-committal yourself, great. But if you mope around waiting for him to call or refuse date invitations from others, this is not good. If you want some certainty, then you need to ask for it. If he's not willing to give it and you're not willing to perpetually be his last-minute date, then you need to let go. Invite him to be your friend, or release him entirely.

Being hooked, no matter how delicious the bait, isn't good for fish or women.

Study shows men go for women with good looks

Duh.

Someone paid good money to fund this study?

Peter M. Todd, Ph.D. and his research team from the cognitive science program at Indiana University, Bloomington, reported this earth-shattering finding in a recent edition of Proceedings of the National Academy of Sciences.

They've come to this monumental conclusion with fewer than four dozen subjects. Their study involved 26 men and 20 women. I guess since we could have told them this information without a study, it doesn't really matter how many subjects there were.

And they were German. The study was done in Munich. And the subjects were reasonably young. Participants ranged in age from 26 to early 40's. Not that if they included older daters the results would have changed appreciably.

Here's how this experiment was conducted. All 46 subjects took part in speed dating — short interactions of three to seven minutes in which people chat. When the allotted time was up, they moved on to meet another dater. Afterward, participants noted from a list the people they'd like to meet again. Dr. Todd said, "Men tended to select nearly every woman above a certain minimum attractiveness threshold." You need a Ph.D. to discover this?

Now, here's the more interesting part: The researchers said women were aware of the importance of their own attractiveness to men, and adjusted their expectations to select the more desirable guys. However, look at how women defined "desirable."

They knew what they could get and aimed for that level.

"Women [selected] men who had overall qualities that were on a par with the women's self-rated attractiveness. They didn't greatly overshoot their attractiveness," Todd said, "because part of the goal for women is to choose men who would stay with them."

Interesting, isn't it, that women innately knew that if a guy was much more attractive than she, he's liable to leave her, no doubt for a woman whose attractiveness more closely matches his. At least this is her assumption.

But, Dr. Todd added, "[The women] didn't go lower. They knew what they could get and aimed for that level."

Women have a sense of their attractiveness level and don't stoop lower. "But," you ask, "how does this explain those homely men with the beautiful women?" It could be he has a lot of money, or he treats her in a way she likes and doesn't get from other men. He could spoil her and shower her with gifts and attention, or he could ignore her and treat her like dirt. It's his behavior in the long run that affects her attraction to him, not his looks.

But in this experiment she wouldn't know how he'd treat her since they met for such a brief period. She mostly had to go by appearance, and women chose men around their same level of attractiveness.

So while we know that men make their choices (at least initially) based on their physical draw to the woman, it is interesting, and perhaps ironic, that the truth is the women's attractiveness influenced the choices for both of them.

Disguised compliments

At an initial dinner date, my guy exclaimed, "Girl, I'm glad you like to eat!" I immediately wondered if I was wolfing down my meal, or if I had ordered too much and he thought I was pigging out. After quickly assessing I'd done neither, I asked what he meant.

Girl, I'm glad you like to eat!"

"A lot of women eat like birds saying they are trying to lose weight. I like to eat and like to be with a woman who enjoys food."

I replied that I liked food and worked to eat consciously, healthily and only until sated. I saw his message was not an insult, but from his perspective, a compliment.

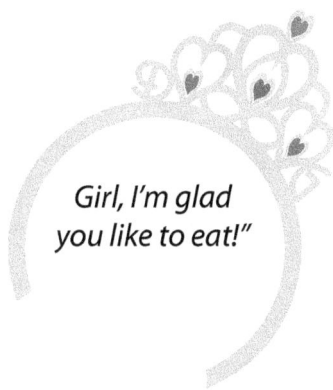

It took me a while to accept that when a man called me "thick" it was not a criticism on being fat, but an appreciative pronouncement on my curves. I've learned that if I think a remark is an insult, but the facial expression and voice tone say otherwise, I need to not get upset, but instead non-defensively ask for clarification. Some terms actually mean the opposite of what you'd initially think. Remember Michael Jackson's song "Bad"? This actually meant "good."

What disguised compliments have you received? What did a date say to you that you at first thought wasn't good, but then learned it was praise?

Getting a man to fall for you

An Adventures in Delicious Dating After 40 reader asked for the trick to getting a man to fall hopelessly and helplessly in love with you. My answer is to paraphrase (with apologies) Mahatma Gandhi's famous quote: "We must become the change we want to see."

My advice:

We must become the woman the man we desire wants to be with.

Now, before you get your Spanx in a knot, I'm not suggesting you become someone you're not. Instead, become the woman who loves yourself so much (not in an arrogant way) that the man you desire can't help but be drawn to you.

Women tend to be so down on themselves, always pointing out the few extra pounds they need to lose, or other "flaws," or talking about the losers they've been dumped by — all while on a date! This is not appealing. Have the confidence to show you like, really like yourself! And those who have similar feelings about themselves will come your way. Your self-assurance will magnetize men who love confident women.

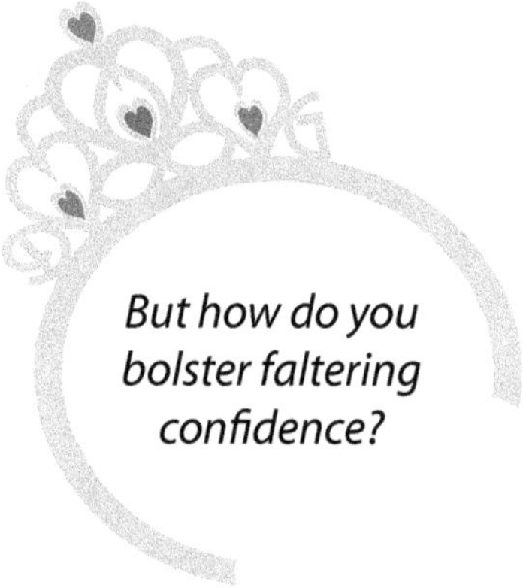
But how do you bolster faltering confidence?

But how do you bolster faltering confidence? Work on the parts of yourself with which you aren't completely happy. Don't telegraph your insecurities to your date — at least in the beginning. Later, when you've built trust and are comfortable being vulnerable, you can share. But it is not alluring to hear someone continually point out their imperfections, especially when the other person doesn't notice them, or if he does, they are inconsequential.

So what could you do to be even more of a man-you-desire magnet?

Do men want feisty women?

I became addicted to "Dancing with the Stars" after several seasons. I know, I'm slow to join the onslaught of rabid fans. What pushed me over the top was Apolo Anton Ohno. What a luscious man! Although he's 30 years my junior, one can still drool, yes? I got so enamored, I spent the evening watching previous DWTS shows at abc.com.

Watching so many shows at once I noticed a theme emerge in the behind-the-scenes interviews with the dancers. The women, at least the ones who stayed in the game, all are strong, confident, and feisty. No surprise here for this highly-competitive sport. But the woman who stands

The women all are strong, confident, and feisty

out for me is Leila Ali, who as a boxing champion one would expect to be strong willed and gutsy. But she mixes it with a sensuality, gracefulness, and allure that have many men's mouths on the floor.

Since many (most?) of my dating gal pals are also spirited, self-assured and spunky, it made me wonder if this was a guy magnet or repellent. While many men are drawn to Leila's beauty and sexuality, is their infatuation only in fantasy form? Or would they actually be drawn to women like that in real life? Since Leila is married, she's obviously found a man who likes her mixture of strength and sensuality.

Many men are intimidated by feisty women. As more women have made our way on our own, either through divorce, widowhood, or life-long singledom, we've had to be strong to survive. Sometimes that strength overrides softness or femininity. We forget how to be sensual. Leila is a great role model for how to exude the perfect balance.

My friend Ava Diamond wrote a powerful book, *Great Quotes from Feisty Women**. She says, "A feisty woman is vibrant, gusty, lives boldly, is true to herself, and embraces her power as a woman." Does this sound like you?

What do you think about feisty women and dating? Is it easier or harder for them/us?

**For info on ordering this book, go to http://www.feisty-women.com*

"What's your favorite curve?"

In "Understanding the stage your guy is in" (page 69) I discussed Alison Armstrong's study of what makes men tick and her subsequent "Celebrating Men, Satisfying Women®" workshops*. I attended the free introductory program and not only confirmed some of what I'd learned on my own, but got some refinements and new information as well.

An interesting concept that I think more women need to hear is that all men don't like the same model-like body shape. In fact, she asked many men, "What's your favorite curve on a woman's body?" Each man grinned as he described and usually drew in the air that curve.

Some were of a woman's breasts or butt, as we'd imagine. But a whole lot more said things like, "The curve where her back transitions to her tush," or "Where her waist goes in under her ribs," or "Where her calf shifts into her ankle." Some men liked the curve of chins, necks, arms, bellies, etc. Who knew? Of course, some men liked more pronounced curves than others.

She also cemented the idea that men look at overall body shape, not individual imperfections. I remember standing naked in the bedroom talking to a boyfriend after taking a shower. He looked me up and down and said, "Wow. I just love your body." Now remember, I am not a gym rat and have bumps and bulges, so this is not what I expected. I pointed to my cellulite-dimpled thighs and said, "So this cottage cheese stuff doesn't bother you?" "No. I don't even notice it." "What about these love handles?" "Nope." I nearly jumped over the king-size bed and kissed him then and there.

I nearly jumped over the king-size bed and kissed him

I've learned that often a man sizes up a woman as his "type" by her shape. That's, in part, how a guy can know if he wants to pursue you or not within seconds of meeting you. It's not only your face, clothes, walk, posture, hair, smell, etc., but much of it is an overall "Do I find her shape attractive." We women usually label that shallow as we think he should get to know our personality before deciding. But it is what it is, and getting angry or frustrated doesn't help really. So having a full-length picture on your dating site profile will eliminate some of those awkward brief meetings when the guy decides you aren't his type within milliseconds.

The good news for us is that no matter what your shape, it's likely some men will find your curves appealing, whether they are prominent or nearly straight. Now if we could just learn to appreciate them as much as the guys do.

* *For info on this workshop, go to http://www.XXX.com*

Make sure to download your free eBook Attract Your Next Great Mate: Dating Advice From Top Relationship Experts *at www. DatingGoddess.com/freebie*

"Men aren't trained in emotions"

Not exactly a news flash.

But since this was uttered by a midlife male pal who I adore, I wanted to hear more on his perspective. He's been dating about three years after his divorce from a long-term marriage. We were talking about why it's so hard for a man to tell a woman he doesn't want to date her anymore, so he just goes poof. Although I've covered this territory with other men, I was interested in his perspective.

"Men are taught to not let their emotions show, through messages like 'Men don't cry,' 'Be tough,' 'Just suck it up.' Men learn to stuff their emotions and freak out when a woman shows hers. So they just disappear rather than having an adult conversation because they don't want to face her potentially crying."

Then he said something that just hit me as brilliant: "Schools ought to have all sixth graders read an age-appropriate version of *Men are from Mars, Women are from Venus*. It would have a huge impact if men and women started understanding the gender's differences early in life, rather than just making the other wrong."

What would life be like if we all got that training early on? Heck, what would your dating life if you only dated men who had read and understood that book, or others like it? Would there be less judgment and more understanding? I think so.

Instead of always finding fault with the other gender, students would learn to appreciate what unique perspectives and attributes the other contributes. There would be less upset and fewer divorces.

Not that John Gray's book is the panacea to peace between the genders. But it is a start. Or perhaps there are others that would be better choices.

Right now we depend on learning about the other gender all on our own. We may read books, talk to wise friends, talk to therapists or take seminars from those who are willing to pass on their knowledge. But we know that many people don't take the initiative to learn on their own. And unfortunately, they never learn and just continue to blame the other gender for being their worst selves.

If you were asked to suggest a book, seminar or resource to another who wanted to learn about gender differences, what would you recommend?

Midlife men have forgotten how to date

Swapping dating stories with a guy pal, I said, based on my observations, it seems many midlife men have forgotten how to date and be with a woman. He agreed. He hasn't been in a relationship in a few years and he's so used to being single he admits he's forgotten some dating skills.

This is from a charming, intelligent, accomplished, good-looking man who's dated a lot since his last long-term relationship three years ago. But he said he wasn't sure what to say when the woman he's been seeing for a few months said, "I'd like us to spend the weekend together." He blurted, "What would we do?" He wasn't sure if they'd run errands together or she was thinking they should go away. He was clueless what they'd do.

I've noticed that a lot of midlife men don't know

how to "date" — meaning how to plan anything beyond movies and dinner. Which is fine occasionally, but they don't seem to know how to plan something more interesting than that — a hike, picnic, concert, comedy club, museum visit, or weekend away. There are even books on ideas for fun, romantic dates, but these guys have either never heard of them or haven't read them.

Why don't men brush up on dating techniques?

Guys also don't seem to understand that women appreciate being asked out a few days in advance. The more days in advance, the more important the woman feels. And the better a woman feels about the man, the more smoothly the date goes. Not that occasional spontaneity isn't fun. But if you only get, "What are you doing in an hour?" phone calls, it makes you feel like you are an afterthought.

It seems that long-single men also seem to have forgotten how to take into consideration what the woman would like. Yes, often they will ask what kind of food I'd like or what movies I want to see, but I've told most dates that I love to dance and only one has taken me dancing — and he did so begrudgingly. (See "Being in step with the dance of dating," in the *Dipping Your Toe in the Dating Pool: Dive In Without Belly Flopping* book). If a man only knew how much mileage he'd get out of doing what I like once in a while!

And of course there are things that most of us would think would be no-brainers — sincere compliments, occasional flowers, basic gentlemanliness (walking on the curb side of the sidewalk, letting the woman go first, helping with a coat, taking a heavy package) and showing you've made some effort to please a woman. I've been surprised at how often these things don't happen, even with educated, accomplished, intelligent, midlife men.

So why don't men brush up on dating techniques before they get back into the dating world? I wish I knew. Women are better at reading books and articles on the subject, or asking friends. Men, I guess, don't think they need to know anything more than what they do. However, they would have much more success in the dating world if they took time to refresh their memory and buff their skills. The object of their affection would be much more enamored with just a refresher of important behaviors.

Entering the Land of Testosterone

I'm experimenting with trying to meet men in the "real" world. I'm inserting myself into places where gobs of possible potential suitors gather. Today I entered the Land of Testosterone.

"Where is that?" you ask.

A professional football game.

A friend had an extra ticket so I attended our local team's game. I thought this would give me an opportunity to be surrounded by enthusiastic men. I was right. But it was not quite what I'd hoped for.

I entered the Land of Testosterone.

Looking around, I assessed potential flirting prospects. I think the vendors must have been selling testosterone-infused beer. The men I observed were fervently cheering our team and vociferously booing the opposition. (To be fair, the women were too.)

The young men around me were taking turns using binoculars to inspect the cheerleaders — who were only 20 feet in front of us. Even with the football players at our end of the field, these voyeurs were more engrossed in scrutinizing the gals' body parts than in watching the plays.

I found myself joining in the oglefest — but my focus was on a fine stud muffin who hovered near the gaggle of cheerleaders by a media video-viewing station. It was unclear what he was doing there, but he had the appropriate credentials to get past security. So when the game got boring, I entertained myself by imaging how I could meet him. After all, he was 25 feet into the secure zone. How would I just bump into him?

But no amount of mental telepathy could get him to saunter up to my third-row seat. I considered calling him over, but I thought that would appear just too desperate. So instead, I just enjoyed the eye candy, but unlike my teenage male row-mates, I didn't use my binoculars.

So I am not having great luck meeting men in places they gather en masse. But I will not give up! I may try a pal's suggestion of car swap meets and car shows. And I may even try NASCAR or boxing — if I get desperate!

Eureka! I have found the answer

Yes, ladies, after much research, I think I've found the answer to how to make a guy fall for you. This has been right in front of our noses for many, many years, and some women have already figured this out. How could I (and perhaps you) be so obtuse?

The secret has been flaunted in nearly every romantic movie we've seen in decades. I've noticed the pattern, but only after recently watching "A Good Year" on DVD did all the puzzle pieces fall into place.

Here it is. Are you ready?

Men fall for women who are mean to them at first.

At least this is the pattern repeated ad nauseam in movies and novels. Take the plot of "A Good Year" for a template. (Spoiler ahead if you don't want to know the movie's ending.)

Man (English, handsome, successful, but jerky) unknowingly runs woman (French, young, slender, beautiful, feisty) off the French country road on her bicycle. She finds him, extracts revenge by not helping him out of a sludge-filled, waterless and ladderless swimming pool into which he's fallen. He is intrigued (while enjoying a peek up her dress from his vantage point). He seeks out woman in town, only to have her display her beautiful derriere in the public square to show him the bruise inflicted in her fall. Fast forward to her accepting a date with him, kissing in the rain, him giving up high-powered job in London to live on ancient estate in Provence with her.

See how simple? I reiterate the formula: be mean to men at first.

Or perhaps you have to be beautiful for this to work, as that is what we see in the movies. You never see an average-looking woman being mean to a guy and him falling for her. Do you? I can't think of any.

See — it's so simple. All a woman has to be is beautiful, then mean to the man, and easy as pie, he falls for her. So all we have to have is movie-star stunningness. Nothing thousands of dollars and countless face lifts, tummy tucks, liposuction, and personal trainers couldn't buy, right? After all, what price love?

But wait — darn, this is fiction. I keep forgetting this, since the messages are so pervasive in so many of our cultural forms: movies, plays, TV, novels. In real life, I know of no long term couples who began because she was mean to him. Or if she was, he was drawn to her hotness first. I'm sure there are some, I'm just saying the vast majority of people who are together didn't start out with an adversarial tone. So I guess *Why Men Love Bitches* can't be our theme.

(Sorry, I was feeling snarky today.)

"Any booty will do"

At my professional association's conference, a long-single man I've known 10+ years stepped up his flirting with me. He's significantly younger, shorter, and geographically undesirable, along with other characteristics that keep us from being a good match, but we're pals and dancing buddies. At one of the informal events, I was lying on my side on the grass talking to some friends. I felt someone slide in behind me to spoon and slip an arm around my waist. It was him.

Although I was surprised, I didn't let on. Since he was a pal, I didn't want to overreact with what I wanted to say, which was: "What the hell are you doing?" I just said hello and continued chatting. I wasn't sure what else to do. After a few minutes, he moved on.

I shared the story with a gal pal later asking for her input to help me understand what happened. Was he just trying to get a quick full-body fix? Was he trying to be flirty? Was this his version of making a pass? Since it was clear to me we weren't a match, was he unclear on this or just playing?

Her insight was priceless. As the mother of two

teenaged boys, she put it in perspective. "My sons tell me, 'Sometimes, Mom, any booty will do.'" Ah, so being pressed up next to a booty — even a fully clothed one — is better than no booty contact. And perhaps he was thinking it might entice me to share more intense booty that night.

I now keep this lesson in mind when I'm finding out about a man before meeting. I want to know how long it's been since his last girlfriend. If more than 6 months, I know he probably hasn't had recent regular affection, so he may feel a bit deprived. (Of course, he could have had a series of short-term booty calls in between.) So I'm a bit more skeptical if he is affectionate on the first few dates, as perhaps he's just trying to scratch a long-overdue itch. I've learned not to take it as a sign that he is besotted with me. I enjoy the attention and affection but try not to read into it, nor let it go too far.

He may feel a bit deprived

Husband in training

A guy pal 10 years my junior was bemoaning that he wanted to be married. *Really* wanted to be married. I asked him some key questions, then announced my diagnosis: he needed to know how to act like a husband. Then the women he dated would see he was ready for marriage. So I adopted him as my Assistant Husband in Training. I was sure my husband wouldn't mind my new project, as long as there were no marital privileges.

We started his training regimen immediately. We were at a professional convention in a downtown hotel. I said, "Let's begin" and slipped my arm through his for a stroll through the surrounding shops.

"Let's go into that jewelry store so we can shop for engagement rings." He complied — he was already being a good trainee! After trying on the biggest diamonds in the store, I chose the one I thought would show his pseudo undying devotion to me and got his agreement. We thanked the jeweler and promised to return later.

In a clothing store he learned to say, "That color brings out your beautiful eyes," "That style would be hot on you," "I'd love to take you to dinner in that outfit," and "Do you need shoes to go with that?" He was a quick study on how to make a woman feel special.

We headed off to lunch. I made sure he knew to open the doors, escort me to the table, pull out the chair, and maintain interested conversation and eye contact. And of course, pick up the bill.

Over the next year we continued our intermittent training program. He'd call periodically and ask how to impress one of his dates. Then he met a woman he decided was a fit, so he wanted suggestions for ways to woo her. I was such a good trainer and he was such a good student, he was married within the year!

Don't you wish the men we date enlisted in boyfriend training, then graduated to husband training? And wouldn't you love to have a mentor teach you how to entice a man and keep him interested for years? Where are such schools? What would you want to see men taught in such a training program, beyond the requisite pick up your wet towels and don't chew with your mouth open?

Signs of manipulation

An Adventures in Delicious Dating After 40 reader asked me to address the topic of manipulation — specifically, how to tell if a man is trying to manipulate you. She says, "I am so gullible and really want to trust so I tend to trust the wrong fellows because I just don't realize how I have been manipulated."

While some of us might think this is common sense, I've found that common sense can quickly fly out the window in affairs of the heart.

The dictionary defines manipulate as "control or influence (a person or situation) cleverly, unfairly, or unscrupulously." It is anytime someone tries to coerce you to do something you don't immediately want to do. However, it goes beyond persuasion, as manipulation is when you've said you don't want to do something and they don't let up.

And for the record, women manipulate, too.

What are the signs?

- ***He doesn't honor your boundaries.*** For example, you're kissing. You're enjoying it. He moves his hand to a place you don't want it. You tell him, "I'm not ready to go there" and move his hand to a place that's okay for you. A few minutes later, he moves it back to where he wants. When you move it again, he says, "I won't go any further" and goes back to where he wanted it. He's manipulating you by discounting your comfort and boundary.

- ***He asks you to do something you feel is unethical or dishonest.*** When you object, he chastises you. When I was dating the psychiatrist, he wanted me to register in person as him for a medical education session so he could get the credit but not have to attend. I refused. He argued. I didn't budge.

- ***He uses affection to coerce you.*** He wants you to do something you don't want to do. He puts his laundry in your hamper. When you protest that you don't want to be doing his laundry, he sidles up next to you, hugs you the way he knows you love and starts kissing your face. "Oh, sweetie, you are such a wonderful woman I didn't think you'd mind doing my little laundry with yours. After all, then our clothes can intertwine, just like we do!"

- ***He bullies you.*** If you say "no," he chides you with, "What are you, a prude?" Or threatens you, "If we don't have sex the next time we're together, I'm history."

- ***He blames you for his not honoring his agreements.*** He promised to take you to the movies.

He gets engaged in the game on TV. You tell him it's time to go, he says, "Just 10 more minutes. We'll still make it." Ten turns into 20. If you say something, you're a nag. If you don't, you miss the movie beginning. He's put you in a double bind — you lose if you say something as well as if you don't. If you miss the movie, he blames you by saying "You should have said something." How about he should have honored his agreement?

- ***He uses guilt to finagle.*** He wants sex. You have a stomach ache. He says, "We never have sex. You always have some excuse. I think you don't love me anymore."

- ***He tries to buy his way.*** "If you attend this wedding as my date, I'll give you $500 for a new dress to wear." (This actually happened to a friend of mine who met a man online who was so desperate for a date to a friend's wedding, he offered her this bribe.)

The bottom line is it's easy to see these as manipulation when you're not in a romance with the person. However, when you are, your clear vision can get cloudy. Hopefully this list will help you be more conscious if any of these happen to you.

What else can you list as ways people manipulate each other? Have you ever manipulated someone? If so, why?

Men and Zen

I dated a vegetarian Buddhist who plays guitar professionally in two Reggae bands. Additionally, he holds down a day job and runs his own small business after hours.

Needless to say, we had interesting conversations. Our first encounter was a hot chocolate date, since neither of us drink coffee. Over frothy cocoa we discussed Buddhist tenets and philosophy, karma, and Reggae vs. R&B music. We compared notes on how to bring a loving and accepting spirit to dating and our businesses. Not the normal first-date conversation. I was drawn to him because of the depth of his thinking, reading and conversation.

Not the normal first-date conversation.

On our second date we rented the sequel to "What the Bleep Do We Know!?," called "Down the Rabbit Hole." On our third date he brought a book on consciousness that we read together and discussed the concepts.

This man is different than any of the others. Rarely have I discussed with a date the concepts of karma, letting go of suffering, predetermination vs. self-determination, evil vs. sickness.

A Buddhist belief is actions have consequences, and his actions drew me to him. Buddhists view nothing as fixed or permanent, so I didn't have the expectation that this relationship would last forever. They also understand that change is possible, so while I didn't try to change him, I noticed how our relationship shifted as we got to know each other better.

The best news is that when we decided not to continue our dating, there was no drama. We both agreed that whatever is is, and since one of us didn't see a future together, then that is what is so. If we continued to date, he wouldn't complain about anything, as he believes in accepting whatever is as perfect. So I could get away with pretty much anything.

But, we decided fate did not have us together long term. So we moved on.

"Men are putty" — sometimes silly putty

A male pal shared that he was dating a new woman. He said he was really drawn to her, because, in part she was into him! Isn't it interesting how attractive someone can become when he or she is attracted to you?

He excitedly shared that she was happy when he called, said she enjoyed spending time with him, and thanked him for his kindnesses. He said this was a departure from the women he's taken out lately. This woman's appreciation made him want to do anything for her. He added, "When we men are appreciated, we're putty."

"When we men are appreciated, we're putty."

Are men really that easy to make into putty? I've never felt I've "puttified" a man, although I do all the things my friend was thrilled about. In fact, some experts tell women to not show appreciation, to be aloof, and make the man work hard for any acknowledgments. I say poppycock. I treat men the way I like to be treated — with kindness, appreciation and care. One man I dated told me, "You're so nice." Another said, "I can't imagine why anyone would ever break up with you." Would that this were true. But it showed that he felt well treated, so he was putty in my hands.

What makes you turn to putty? I know what melts my heart. It's not big things, but cumulative little things. Make a list of what you love, from kisses on the back of your neck, to help bringing in groceries, to chivalrous acts. Ask your man to do the same. Then swap lists so you know how to make the other happy.

When we are happy and feel appreciated we all can let our fun-loving selves out to play. Then we can become silly putty!

Are you getting prime time from your man?

A guy pal called me on a Friday night and was surprised I was home. He knew I'd been dating a guy for a few weeks and thought I'd be out on the town. "Is he out of town?" he asked. "No." When I explained that I saw my guy Wednesday, but we weren't scheduled to see each that weekend, my friend gently suggested this wasn't a good sign.

"If he hasn't locked you up for a weekend date, he's not thinking this relationship is 'A' priority. If he is kicking with his buds on Friday and watching the game on Saturday night — without you — this isn't good. You're not at the top of his priority list." He was right.

I now watch for what days a guy asks to see me and how far in advance he asks for the date. If he only wants to see me during the work week and not the weekend, a yellow flag unfurls. If he waits until the last minute to call, it seems that he's seeing if something better comes along. If nothing does, he gives me a call. I don't want to play hard to get; I also don't want to be at his beck and call. While I don't mind a spontaneous date once in a while, I really appreciate when someone puts some thought into making sure I'll be available in advance.

Notice when he calls to chat. Is it always on his way to or from work? Walking to a meeting? Cleaning his house? Watching TV? Then he's multitasking. I know, we are all busy nowadays, but if he's doing something else, he's not fully available to talk about — and listen to — important things. He's probably just "reporting in" and wanting a superficial conversation. While those are fine for short talks, I want some focused time to talk about deeper subjects.

Notice where you fit in his priorities

So notice where you fit in his priorities. Once I made a first call at an agreed upon time. The guy's first words after "hello" were, "Can I call you back? I have to put the towels in the linen closet." How important do you think that made me feel? Putting away his laundry was more important than talking to me. Although I saw him periodically over six months, that first observation held true throughout. He was always busy doing other things so he had little time for me — other than talking to me while he was driving somewhere other than to see me!

I've been told that if you only get mid-week dates and last minute calls, you may be his "spare" girlfriend.

In other words, there's an alpha gal who gets weekend time, and you get the leftovers. Same with phone calls — if he's calling you mostly while in the car, maybe he's got a live-in so can't talk at home. Not that one should be overly suspicious, but don't be a chump. Learn some of the signs so you know what you're getting yourself into. If you, too, are balancing two guys, you can't really complain.

If you notice he's not giving you prime time, then talk to him about it. If he refuses to give you "A" time, then move on.

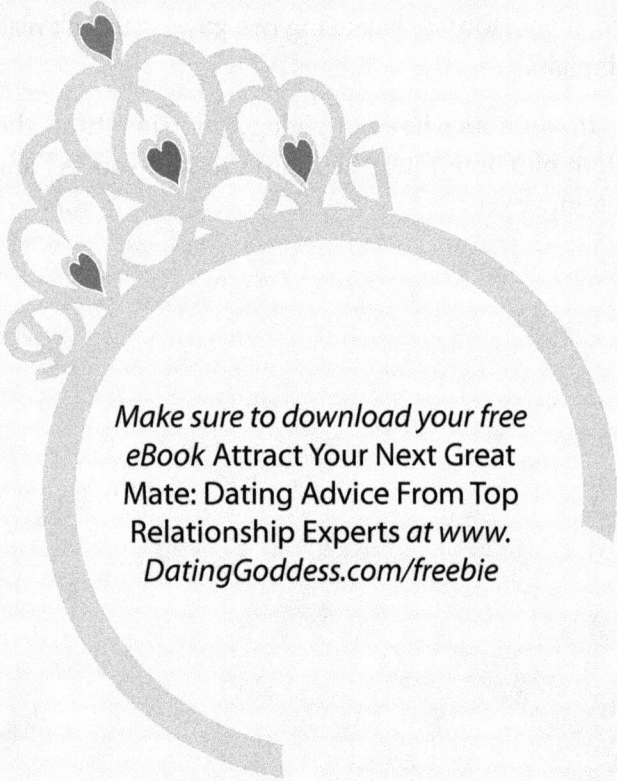

Emotional unavailability

Many of the women I've talked to say they've dated men who were emotionally unavailable. I realized I'm not sure how to tell if a guy is emotionally available or not. So I did a little research.

An article at Neil Rosenthal's Heart Relationships site* listed a number of ways to tell if someone is emotionally unavailable. After reading the list, I would say that a good deal of the men I've gone out with had at least one sign!

So does this mean that I attract men who are emotionally unavailable, or there is an inordinate percentage of the unattached men — at least listed on dating sites — who have this affliction? If the latter, is this why they are single?

One of the signs Rosenthal lists is "They're too busy, sick, tired or preoccupied with other things. Their energy, time and life-force are all taken with other priorities." Many midlife people — both men and women —

seem to have already full lives. In "Dating takes time" (in the book *Date or Wait: Are You Ready for Mr. Great?*) I talked about how surprised I have been with men who profess to want to date, yet have a hard time fitting in dinner or a movie between work, kids, parents, working out, friends, and other life maintenance. So is this lack of time for establishing a relationship because of their overextended lives, or because of emotional unavailability?

And how do we know that we aren't the ones who are emotionally unavailable? What are the signals that you are emotionally available?

What are the signs you've seen that point to emotional unavailability?

* For Neil's article go to http://www.heartrelationships.com/ARTICLES/SabotagingaRelationship/Sept-17SabotagingRelationshihp.htm

When a man tells you what he paid for things

For two months I dated a man who told me what he paid for his Mercedes ($85,000), his Ferragamo shoes ($450), his Persian rug ($1400), his Rolex ($10,000), and his son's PlayStation ($600), among other items. He was a wealthy man who spent less than $100 total on our weekly dates.

This got me wondering what was up. Was he not that into me that he only took me to dinner twice (including once to Chili's) and out to the movies once? The rest of the time it was a simple dinner at his house or mine and a DVD. Oh, yes, there was the debacle of taking me dancing where he spent $26 for our admission, then declined to dance with me, but wouldn't leave because he'd paid the entrance fee and wanted to stay until he got his money's worth.

Was he just stingy? Tightfisted? Miserly? I can understand if someone is frugal, especially if they live on a modest income, but why the incongruence between what he spent on himself and what he spent on our entertainment? While I didn't expect him to spend exorbitantly on our dates, nor do I need a wealthy man, the disparity was glaring.

So why do some men feel the need to tell you how much they spent on their toys? I think it is so they can prove they are successful. It is the same reason they wear logo shirts (e.g., Ralph Lauren) and Rolex watches, to give the aura of affluence. However, they could also be up to their eyeballs in hock to afford these luxuries. I call it affluent poverty when someone goes into debt to appear they are financially successful. I'd much prefer seeing last year's tax return, net worth balance sheet and 401k statement than high-end cars, watches, or shoes.

I think continually boasting about the price of your acquisitions reeks of low-self esteem. It shows you are trying to impress someone with your purchasing power. This man grew up lower middle class and worked himself to the top of his profession. I guess the way to show he had made it — not only to himself but to others — was to buy himself expensive toys, and of course, to tell others what he paid for them.

Continually boasting about the price of your acquisitions reeks of low-self esteem.

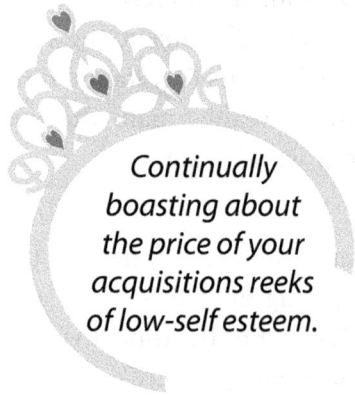

However, many people who have learned to like fine purchases also take pleasure in sharing similar items with people of whom they are fond, whether family, friends, or women they are wanting to woo. While I helped him choose generous Christmas gifts for acquaintances, I got nothing, not even a card. For Valentine's Day again I received not a thing — not even a call, although I sent him a card and he promised to take me to dinner. It never happened. That's when I decided I didn't want to date a wealthy, bragging Scrooge.

When a man repeatedly tells you what he spent on things, note the yellow flag. And if he then spends virtually nothing on you, run the other direction.

Understanding the stage your guy is in

Alison Armstrong began her study of what makes men tick in 1991 and her staff gives "Celebrating Men, Satisfying Women®" workshops around the country. Her focus is on creating peace and partnership between men and women.

She shares some of her findings in her novel, *Keys to the Kingdom*. The novel format makes the information easy to digest. In fact, you don't really mind that she repeats the same information in different words because one character is telling someone new. It's a non-annoying way to review the concepts.

What are those concepts? She focuses on the stages of men's development from birth to old age, how to tell what stage they are in, and how to deal with them effectively at each stage. When a woman doesn't understand what's going on with the men in her life, it is easy to be frustrated, hurt and angry. And to make matters worse, most men don't understand what is happening for them, so they can't explain it to the women they love.

The stages' names are based on medieval terms:

- ***Page:*** Birth to puberty. "Wannabe Knights"; they want adventure on their (a child's) scale.
- ***Knight:*** Puberty until late twenties/early thirties. Characterized by a drive for adventure, fun, challenge, passion.
- ***Prince:*** Late twenties/early thirties through 40-45ish. Focus is on who he wants to be in his life, what he wants to accomplish, and goes about bringing that to bear, even at the neglect of his wife and family, even though he says (and truly believes) he is working this hard for their benefit.
- ***King:*** 40+. Kings are confident of who they are. They may not have acquired a lot of material wealth, but they are generous, whether with gifts, time, attention or affection.
- ***Elder:*** Later years, near the end of his life. Not all men become Elders. A man's life is complete. There is nothing to do but enjoy life, explore what he's curious about, appreciate his blessings and serve humanity.

There's also a "state" — not really a stage — called "The Tunnel" which most of us would label midlife crisis. This occurs during the transition between Prince and King. A man questions what he's achieved and become, and can be dissatisfied at this point. He can then become withdrawn, difficult, uncommunicative, and a challenge to be around.

I am not doing these explanations justice, but wanted to give you a flavor of the concepts. She describes each one much better and in more depth, and what women can do to effectively communicate with men who are in the various stages.

Alison's belief, as explained through her characters, is that incorporating this information into your behavior with the men around you transforms your relationship to all men for the better.

Based on the age of most of my potential suitors, they should be in the "King" stage, but I've found many of them to behave like they are in the "Knight" stage — wanting adventure and fun, with no maturity about — or perhaps just not the desire to do — what it takes to be in a relationship. So I don't think we should hold the age ranges as gospel. I'm wondering if maybe men can revert to a previous stage, based on their life circumstances. So, for example, after a divorce, with their newfound freedom, they are feeling more Knight-like, at least when it comes to relationships. She didn't address this in the book.

I took the 3-hour introduction to the "Celebrating Men, Satisfying Women®" workshops, which is called "Making Sense of Men™" and found some of the concepts instructive. Alison has found a way to organize some of the information many of us know into a useful context and format. For more info, go to www.understandmen.com.

Does he treat you like his ex?

The question is really, "Does the guy you're dating treat you like he treated his ex wife?" Not the way he currently treats his ex wife, as he could treat her better or worse than when they were together. But does he behave the way he did when they were together?

Let me give you an example. I was wooed by a man who lives 400 miles away. He called me every day for 4 months before we met. Finally, he flew to meet me and got a hotel room for the weekend. We enjoyed a variety of activities that weekend as we got to know each other face to face.

Several weeks later I needed to be in his city for business, so he invited me to stay with him afterward. Now on his turf, I saw he went about his activities as if I wasn't really there. He turned on the TV and watched it as we had drinks and he cooked dinner. It stayed on the rest of the evening. So much for talking and getting to know each other. It was still on when I plodded off to the guest room, as he used it to put himself to sleep.

It kept me awake.

The next day he preferred to watch TV than to accept my invitation for a walk. When I arrived back at his condo, he was engrossed in a sports event so wasn't interested when I suggested going out for a movie.

I surmised that this is not only what he does when he is alone, but most likely what he did when he was married. His wife was not someone with whom he had much desire to interact, unless it was about their college-aged son. They ignored each other unless she insisted they talk about something. Based on what he told me, they mostly went their separate ways unless a dinner with friends required their joint presence.

This was how he thought relationships should be, so he treated his dates like this too. I was not someone whom he was interested in getting to know — just someone to have around at his convenience.

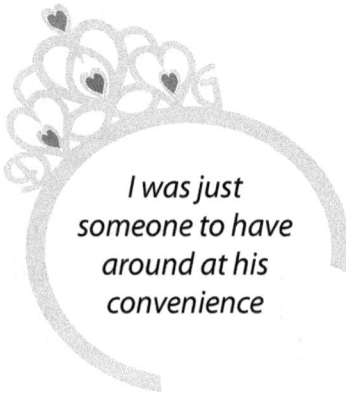

I was just someone to have around at his convenience

So if a guy treats you in a way you consider odd, ask yourself if it could be that this is how he treated his ex. Some men don't learn to think about how the woman he's dating would like to be treated. He treats her the same as his ex. The guy in the example wasn't unintelligent, he was just not astute.

And examine your own behavior as well. Do you tend to treat your suitors similarly to how you treated your ex? I know I have. It takes awareness to craft how to get along with each man independently, rather than lumping them all into the "what men like" basket.

What have you observed about how you might habitually treat your dates similarly to how you treated your ex? And how have you broken yourself of that habit?

Has Greg Behrendt done women a disservice?

You may know that Greg Behrendt is the more visible co-author, with Liz Tuccillo, of the wildly popular advice book for women, He's Just Not That Into You. In it they tell us, among other things, that if a man you're dating doesn't call you at least once a day, he's just — you guessed it — not that into you.

Additionally, if a man's not asking to see you at least once a week, he's not that drawn to you, as other things are taking his focus.

If you believe the book — as I have in the past — you have used how frequently a man contacts you to determine how into you he is. If he doesn't call, text, IM or email at least every couple of days, nor ask me out at least once a week — ideally by Wednesday (a la *The Rules*), I've decided he's not into me and continue dating other guys.

There are several problems with this premise:

- In the beginning, a man may like you but not be

head-over-heels smitten. He's not sure how into you he is. Yes, there are some who are infatuated at a first encounter — or sometimes even before. But there are many who need a bit more time together to decide they want to woo you.

- Some (many?) men are single focused. If they are traveling, away on business, or just engrossed in a project, they may think of you, but not when it's convenient to call. If his business travel is as chaotic as mine often is, I'm on the go from 6:30 a.m. until I fall into bed. When I think of my guy it may be while I have a pause during a seminar, but it isn't appropriate to call. When there is a break, it is taken up by bio needs, interacting with participants, and returning business calls. When I get back to my room, I'm pooped so I respond to important emails, have room service, and fall into bed. I'm sure many guys are the same.

- Some guys just don't like to talk on the phone, so they avoid it. They'll call to set something up with you, but not to chat. So you may only talk on the phone once or possibly twice a week. Maybe he's more of a texter, IMer or emailer than a talker. Or if he texts you more than calls then it may be because he can get away with a surreptitious text during a day-long boring meeting, but he can't get away long enough for a call.

- Guys haven't read Greg and Liz's book so they don't know what is expected of them. They haven't been trained on how they are supposed to

> behave to show a woman he's into her. Even if he has read it, he may decide that calling once a day in the first few weeks seems like stalking and he doesn't want to frighten you away. So he makes his own decision about what seems reasonable.

When a man says he's smitten by me yet he doesn't call every day or ask to see me every week, I've learned to bring it up with him so we can clarify my expectations (thanks to the book) versus his behavior. If after a month or so, we don't talk every day or two — even when I initiate some of the calls — I want to know if he's not feeling it and we should just move on. I begin, "The book *He's Just Not That Into You* may have led me astray. It says if a man is into you he'll call every day. I know you've said you are smitten by me, but we only talk every few days. Is that more your comfort level than every day? I would like to touch base every day, but I'm also willing to adapt my expectations." I've been pleased with the conversation that this has spawned.

The book He's Just Not That Into You *may have led me astray*

So while I think the book did a huge service to women who make up excuses for guys who have gone poof never to return, not all of the advice is relevant regarding all men. We must be willing to interpret each man's behavior based upon that man's motivations, life style and preferences, and not lump them all together. We'd hate it if someone said, "All women...." I don't have many behaviors that are stereotypically associated with women. I don't like to shop, for example. So I get irritated if someone tries to pigeonhole me. We shouldn't do that to guys either.

What's your definition of "independent"?

The term "independent woman" is often seen in men's profiles who seek self-sufficient women. It is their way of saying they want a woman who has a life of her own, interests, friends, a career and sufficient income. They don't want someone who is clingy, reliant on them for all entertainment and definitely not someone they would need to support financially.

However, I have a new understanding of some men's definition of "independent." In addition to the above, it can mean "a woman who doesn't need much from me in terms of a relationship. We can both come and go as we please, and hook up when the whim strikes. Little communication needs to occur between hook ups. I don't want to put much time or energy into the relationship. Hey, we're both busy people."

I would never have guessed that this was part of one's definition of "independent." However, the Thesaurus offers these words: unconnected, disinterested, uncommitted, detached and unconstrained. Unfortunately, these words more closely describe my relations with a man I dated for months who repeatedly said he appreciated my independence.

His definition of independent apparently was that he would call me when he wanted, occasionally text me, see me when the whim struck, and maybe return my calls and maybe not. When it struck me that his definition of independent and mine were vastly different, I saw that his was self-absorbed. While I am independent in the traditional definition, I also think I am considerate of others.

Discovering different definitions can be jarring.

If a man says he wants an independent woman, ask him to further define it to make sure you are on the same page. If not, discovering different definitions can be jarring.

When you hear that a man wants a woman who's independent, what does that mean to you? Have you ever discovered that your definition and his were very different? If so, how?

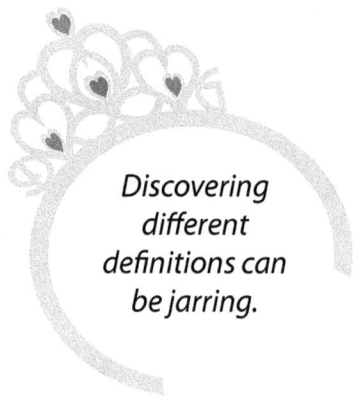

Tales of woo

I was surprised this week to hear from an out-of-the-area man who called me several times a week for a month a few months ago. We'd had a nice connection and he said he wanted to come see me soon, then he went AWOL with an occasional cryptic email. He'd told me he removed himself from the dating site because he'd found me and wasn't interested in anyone else.

I'd texted him a few times and called to make sure he was OK, but got nothing back. I figured he'd found someone else, probably someone local, which was fine, although I did like our chats.

In his recent cryptic email, he said something about "the one I'm after now." I said it was fine if he was pursuing another woman, I'd just like to know so I wouldn't bother him with emails or texts. He responded, "You are the one I'm after."

This made me scratch my head. How can a man possibly think that an occasional one-line email is pursuing?

He's not the first who has made me question a man's definition of wooing or pursuing. Some think that a once a week phone call — with no plan to get together — is sufficient. Others think regular emails, IMs or texts are pursuing. What happened to an actual date? And on that date, more than take out and watching a DVD?

I've been wooed in ways that felt to me like wooing — regular connection, filled with sweet talk on both sides and plans put forth to get together. Romantic cards — real and virtual, flowers, small gifts, a plan for a fun date, these all feel like elements of wooing. A man striving to make a positive impression, wanting to curry my favor through acts — even small acts — this seems like wooing to me.

How could a man think he's pursuing a woman who he barely contacts? I think it is all just smoke.

Romance takes finance

I dated a man for 6 months who was going through financial difficulty. When I asked why we didn't see each other more than once every 10 days or so, he said he didn't want to see me without being able to take me out. I explained that I was more interested in getting to know him than on his ability to entertain me. He said, "Romance takes finance."

His comment has come back to me, especially during this time of financial uncertainty. Some men who began flirting with me have put off plans to meet after getting laid off or had personal economic downturns. Others shared that their financial struggles have affected their confidence in their abilities to woo a woman.

While I'm clear I don't want to be with a man who's got a lot of financial baggage, if a man interests me I'm willing to make allowances for short-term economic woes. Typically, I let a man suggest activities that are comfortable for him, since most midlife men have wanted to treat for entertainment, especially during the wooing stage. I am fine if he suggests getting together for coffee, a walk, video, etc. I will also suggest no- or low-cost activities, like hikes, bike riding, museum visits, movie rental, cooking a meal together, picnics, and playing a game at home. Some have offer their own frugal activities, or I've offered to treat for some.

Women need to be sensitive to a man's economic status without probing so it makes him uncomfortable. But if he says, "What would you like to do this weekend?" and you suggest the hottest play in town, with an expensive dinner beforehand, he may not feel comfortable telling you he can't afford it. You can suggest you pay for one activity, but some won't be comfortable with that either.

So if a man I'm starting to see asks what I want to do, I'll say, "Give me some options you think would be fun" to let him suggest activities he can afford. If he says, "I'd like to do what you think would be fun," I'll offer a range activities: "We could go for a hike, try the new Chinese restaurant, see the hot new movie, attend that new play, or rent a DVD and cook dinner together." Then I let him choose the one that feels right to him.

The point is to be sensitive to a man's pocketbook. He doesn't want to tell you he's having financial problems, so don't make him share that until he is comfortable doing so. Don't assume he'll wine and dine you at the best places unless he offers to do so. Offer to cook or take him out once in a while.

Why men don't tell you you're pretty

Some men tell you they think you are attractive on the first or other early dates. Some will never tell you.

For two months I dated a man who never said he thought I was attractive. In frustration at his aloofness, one day I said to him, "I don't even know if you find me attractive." He said, "I'm pursuing you, aren't I?" Since I didn't consider this wealthy man's once-a-week phone calls and occasional casual, home cooked meals much of a pursuit, I retorted, "Are you?" In other words, he didn't feel he needed to tell me he was attracted to me or thought I was pretty or sexy. His actions -- minimal as they were -- should speak for themselves. So I guess he found me minimally attractive. Or he never learned to express himself to a woman in a way that would make her feel good.

Upon sitting down for dinner with another man for a first encounter, he looked at me, paused, and said, "You're beautiful." I smiled and said, "Thank you." That was the last time I heard it for several months. When he uttered it again, I said, "Thank you. That feels good to hear." He said, "I don't tell beautiful women they are beautiful." When I asked, "Why not?" he said, "Beautiful women know they are beautiful and they hear it all the time. It doesn't mean anything to them because so many people tell them. Average-looking women know they aren't beautiful, so if you tell them they are, they know you are lying. And women think that someone wants something from them if you compliment their looks. So I find it best to not tell women they are beautiful, pretty or sexy."

Can you imagine? Yes, I know you can, but I'm guessing you're as incredulous as I am about these attitudes.

So what about those of us who aren't classically beautiful? Using the last guy's logic, since he finds you beautiful, you must hear this all the time and have grown weary of hearing it. But if you have the kind of attractiveness that some find pretty and others find average, I bet you don't feel you hear "You're very pretty" too many times.

I think some men hold back telling a woman she is beautiful (or pretty or sexy) because they don't want to come across as fawning, smarmy, unctuous or gushy. He doesn't want a woman to think he has fallen for her based only on her looks, so then can be led around by his nose. When some women know a man is ga-ga for her, they use it to manipulate him. It's happened for eons.

And of course, men can use these compliments as a "line" to get closer to you. As I discussed in "He had me from 'You're gorgeous!'"[1] I was enamored with this guy from the get-go, but his salutation was only part of the enticing package. But alas, his thinking (or at least saying) I was gorgeous was not enough to keep him around after three dates. He went poof.

Intellectually we know that it only matters that we think we are attractive, and what others think isn't our concern. But deep down we also like to know that the person we are dating finds us attractive and is able to express that genuinely. Yes, it can be overdone so that you think the man only wants to be with you because of your looks. But if he tells you sincerely and regularly, somehow it makes him more attractive too! And, of course, the more beautiful a person is on the inside, as shown through his thoughtfulness, kindness, caring, respect and attention toward you and others, his outer looks become more appealing. (See "Yummy is as yummy does."[1])

How do you feel when a man tells you sincerely he thinks you're attractive (beautiful, pretty, sexy)? And what have you done when a man you've gone out with for more than a month is stingy in this area?

[1]Both these pieces are from the *First-Rate First Dates: Increasing the Chances of a Second Date* book

Are women's emotions bought too easily?

I watched Steve Harvey promote his book, *Act Like a Lady, Think Like a Man* on Oprah. Steve talked about how women give "it" up to men too easily, without making the man earn it. And a man doesn't respect anything he doesn't have to earn.

By "it" Steve meant not only sex, but a woman's heart. I've read this in other sources too. One man bragged about how easily he could get a woman to forgive him for some selfish act. "Just bring her a $5 bouquet and she gets all gooey eyed. Or just beg her to forgive you over the phone and you don't even have to spring for flowers!"

I'm afraid these men are right a lot of the time. A man can treat us horribly and if he says or does the right things in the moment, we forgive him. He may or may not promise to ever repeat the behavior. And even if he does promise to clean up his act, he doesn't have to follow through as he knows the next time it happens, he can cheaply buy his way back into our hearts — and beds.

I've experienced this myself even though I know better. If a man with whom I am smitten has done something disrespectful, selfish, or uncaring yet apologizes profusely, I've forgiven him. If he tops it with words of undying devotion, even better. And if this apology is punctuated with flowers, yep, I'm usually a goner. And often he is a goner — as in gone — before too long, by exiting himself. His apologies were a ruse to stick around until he was done with me.

Why do we let our emotions be bought so easily?

Why do we let our emotions be bought so easily? Why don't we insist a man show us his ardor through his repeated actions of caring, not just short-term fixes?

I think so many women long for a loving connection that we interpret small actions as signs of long-term devotion. We don't let the scenario play out for a bit to see if he is consistent in showing his interest and earning a place in our heart.

Have you let your emotions be bought easily in the past? If so, what did you learn to not repeat?

Are you teaching what you need to learn?

You may not be a teacher per se, but we teach by what we advise others. If you've been dating for any time, you have no doubt given a friend advice on a situation s/he's facing.

In writing these missives, I've become clear that what I suggest to you is often the lesson I need for myself. In fact, sometimes I write a posting not so much for you, my dear readers, but to cement the learning in my own psyche.

Today a teacher appeared for me. The irony of the encounter was so glaring I knew it was a lesson for me as well.

He'd contacted me via email a year ago, but I was not a member of the site so could not respond. His email was fine, but not so compelling that it motivated me to join the site to reply.

Yesterday, he emailed a long message commenting on specific things he liked in my profile and what we had in common. I'm still not a member of the site, so couldn't respond, but he included his phone number. I thought a man who'd gone to this much trouble deserved at least a brief phone call.

In his profile he stated he had two masters degrees in behavioral sciences and led seminars in interpersonal communication. Since I lead seminars in that area myself, I thought we might click.

On the phone we began by chatting about his quick recovery from major surgery last year. We transitioned into his months-long project that resulted in a book deal. He conducted communication seminars around the country, which included listening skills, because "listening is so important to good communication, and I'm a very good listener. After all, I learn nothing when I'm speaking and I want to know about the other person." Which lead to how he'd … and then he'd … which got him to … and now he's….

Do you see a pattern here?

Do you see a pattern here?

Periodically, I interjected when he took a breath and added my brief comments. None of them resulted in any follow up questions. After 15 minutes, when he finally asked me, "So what do you like to do for fun?" I was relieved that he finally cared to know at least something about me. I replied, "I have eclectic tastes and like to do a variety of activities depending on my mood and who's available to share them." I was ready to start listing some of these various activities, when he interrupted, "Do you like to go to wine, er, wine, ah, wine festivals, art museums or lectures?" Before I could respond he was off and running with more on himself and what he liked to do.

I'm learning to limit my time with folks who seem to only enjoy monologues. So after 20 minutes of him learning nothing about me, I said I needed to go. Ironically, we had a lot of things in common. Unfortunately, he wasn't interested in hearing what those were.

So how is this person who claims to value listening and interpersonal communication a teacher for me/us? It was a reminder to monitor my own listening and communication skills. Am I engaging the other person as much as I could? Do I deliver a monologue? Am I as conscious as I could be of making sure to share air time?

What is it that you advise others that is really a reminder for you? Sometimes it's the behaviors in which we think we are strong that really need the most work.

What shape do men find attractive?

Of course, each man has his own "type." But the research shared in the Discovery Channel program, "The Science of Sex Appeal" gives us some generalizati ns.

In the program, a cross section of men rated the sex appeal of various computer-generated women's silhouettes. (They didn't alter the bust size so that had minimal influence on their choices.) The shape that was deemed the most appealing by the majority of men had a waist to hip ratio of .7. The ratio of a 24 waist to 36 hips is .66. The smaller the ratio the better, meaning the more pronounced the difference. It's not surprising that the Barbie doll's ratio is 5.4. Ll'l Kim is the best example of a famous woman with a pronounced ratio, at least by my estimation. Then perhaps Beyonce.

We would then assume that small-waisted, large-hipped women would be the rage, at least among the general male population, however this is clearly the ideal for some specialized groups. But they are not what is shown in the media as alluring for the masses. Supermodels have trimmer hips than this ratio.

Why do men find this shape so appealing? Evolutionary biologists believe is has to do with men being attracted to women with large enough hips to easily give birth, thus more likely to have his offspring survive. If her hips are too small, there's a higher chance something could go wrong during childbirth.

The good news for midlife dating women is many of us now hove broader hips than when we were younger. So if your waist is relatively smaller, you should be in high demand!

My next boyfriend will be a bellman!

Arriving home tonight from an 11-day international trip, I lifted my heavy bags into my trunk at the airport. It occurred to me that I'd schlepped these bags more than I cared to when help was not on the horizon. It made me appreciate the cheerful van drivers, bellmen and skycaps who did offer to hoist my bags.

I began to ruminate on the many things men — often strangers — do to lighten women's burdens. Not only luggage lifting, but I've been struck by how often men have gone out of their way to give directions or even walk me to my destination. Sure, some of them have been in a role at a hotel, but many have not. They were just helpful strangers. I think the more we women are willing to accept their aid, the more willing men are to go out of their way. This has nothing to do with being a helpless woman. It has to do with being a grateful recipient to someone's kindness. Did I need the hotel banquet staffer to escort me to the door of the ladies room? No. Pointing it out would have been sufficient. But I didn't waive him off with an "I can find it," instead allowing him to feel the satisfaction of completing his task.

Arriving in Manila at 5:30 a.m., I stopped at the airport information desk to ask about storing my luggage so I could catch a town tour during my 16-hour layover. Discovering there were no lockers and I couldn't check my bags into my connecting airline for 14 hours, I had few alternatives. The young information desk clerk helped me see the most viable option was to rent a small room at the airport Day Lounge. I could lock my bags there, or take advantage of the bed and shower to rest during the long layover.

He could have given me directions, but instead opted to call a colleague to cover his desk and escort me. While navigating the labyrinth of elevators, security checkpoints and behind-the-scenes hallways, I was appreciative he'd taken the time. Several times he negotiated in Tagalog with Security and other gatekeepers. When we arrived at the nearly hidden Day Lounge I heaped thanks on him.

When a man offers assistance — whether it's help with a heavy box or directions — do you accept readily? Or do you cut him off, saying, "I've got it"? If the latter, consider that you could actually give him a gift by accepting his

Do you cut off
a man's offer of
assistance?

offer. You both get to experience the generosity of the other.

That's not to say you can't offer to assistance, too. When I travel, I often see one in a party taking a picture of the other(s). I now make it a habit to offer to take a picture of everyone together. During this trip, a large military convention was in town. In the mall, military men from dozens of countries were enjoying the music and people watching. Cameras were flashing non-stop. As I came upon these groups, I made my offer. No one refused. I felt good for contributing to their memories by allowing the whole party to be in the pic. I felt like I'd connected to them in a way that otherwise wouldn't have happened. And who knows, maybe I left a positive impression of Americans in my wake.

The lesson is to not be stingy in either your receiving or your giving. Both are a gift. Be sure to express your appreciation. Even if you can heft your own bags yourself, thank you very much, allow a man to contribute to you.

Different definitions of "pursue"

Webster's dictionary says "pursue" means: "seek to form a sexual relationship with (someone) in a persistent way."

I explained in "Tales of woo" how some men's definition of "pursue" seems skewed to me. Another example has occurred this week.

A few weeks ago a local man showed signs of interest. We emailed a few times, then I gave him my number and we had several long, interesting chats. The only problem was he was on a business trip and wouldn't be returning until after I left for SE Asia. I suggested he download Skype so we could continue our voice chats.

While I was gone, there was no communication. No voice mails, no emails. And no Skype, so he didn't follow through by downloading it.

The evening I was to return home, I got this email:

"Missing you bad; the conversation is invigorating

and the woman is scintillating. I hope things are good for you there. Let's talk soon."

I responded that I would be home the next day and we could chat while I drove home from the airport, but it might be too late for him, so let me know. When I arrived home there was no voice mail so I called him. I got his voice mail so left a message. I've not heard a peep from him in almost a week since he sent the "Missing you bad" email.

What gives? Too busy to make contact? I don't buy it. Found someone else? Maybe. Not that into me? Then why write an email like that?

I continue to scratch my head trying to understand why men do and say certain things, then don't take any action. My cynical self thinks he's juggling several women and I'm not at the top of his list. Or maybe he's married.

Have you "marked" your man?

I'd posted a brief, "I'm glad you're in my life" message to my then-beau's social networking page after we were exclusive for four months.

He said, "I feel like a fire hydrant."

"What do you mean?" I asked curiously.

"I feel marked."

Wow! I hadn't thought I had posted anything personal. No reference to our dating. No pictures of us snuggling. Nothing I wouldn't have posted to a dear friend's site.

Yet he felt I was claiming him as mine to the world. Which, since we'd been dating for 4 months exclusively, I thought he was. But that wasn't really the purpose of my message. It was just to write something warm to him. Okay, and I thought it was a subtle way to tell all the women sending him love messages and scantily clad pictures that I was actually in his life, and they just wanted to be.

I didn't imagine my gesture would be interpreted negatively. After all, within weeks of our dating, he had a server take out picture cuddling in a restaurant, then kissing. He then posted these pics to his Flickr page for all his family and friends to see. He didn't ask my permission to do so, and if he had, I would have been flattered and said "yes."

Another friend shared he'd felt marked by his then-girlfriend of 6 months. She posted pictures of them cuddling during a weekend getaway. He considered these intimate pictures that he didn't really want shared with her 700 and his "friends" 500. He said he was a private person and he'd have shared them with his inner circle via email. He resented her posting them without his permission. He felt it was her way of marking him and letting the world know he was hers.

This has given me new perspective on what the people we're dating are comfortable sharing with the world and what they aren't. I once posted a blog piece announcing a dinner date's amazing accomplishment, including his name. (This is the only time I've listed any date's name.) I thought he would like getting a little more publicity. I was wrong! He was livid that I'd posted it as he didn't want people to know about his personal life, including who he'd taken out to dinner.

Have you been publicly marked? If so, how did you feel? Did he let you know ahead of time, or were you surprised? If you'd marked someone you're dating, how did he react?

Understanding testosterone's impact on dating over 40

Have you considered how much testosterone impacts our dating lives? And for that matter, our lives in general? Since both men and women have testosterone, I was interested in Public Radio International's "This American Life" show called "Testosterone" last year. It was a fascinating listen.

A man who stopped producing testosterone due to a medical treatment described life without the hormone. Unlike his normal, testosterone-filled life, he saw everything as beautiful. His objectivity sharpened. His criticalness declined. His desire for anything — food, work, sex — reduced dramatically.

In another interview, Griffin Hansbury, who started life as a woman and now lives as a man, shared his experience of taking massive testosterone injections seven years ago. He explains how testosterone changed his views on nature vs. nurture.

Griffin said the most overwhelming feeling was increased libido and desire for sex. His mind flooded with aggressive pornographic images when seeing even mildly attractive women. Everyday things turned erotic. Erections came easily. He said he felt like a monster that he couldn't control. His inner feminist dialog commonly fought with his macho instincts.

What if, as Griffin explains, men are hard pressed to control these actions? Griffin has the advantage of having lived life as a woman and knows how it feels to be on the receiving end. He has sensitivity to feeling disrespected and treated like a sexual object. Yet with all that insight, he still found he was challenged not to think obscene thoughts about women he encountered on the street or subway. So if he fought the thoughts, what chance does a man have who isn't so aware?

This program helped explain why man some men do what they do. Women often denigrate men's behavior — especially around unseemly sexual comments or approaches. "What a jerk." "What a sleezeball." "What a dirty old man." How about: "This man clearly doesn't understand what is socially appropriate."

Smart men learn to not express their sexual thoughts aloud in inappropriate settings. Yet some cannot control the physical sensations they get from being around a woman who turns them on. They can only stay seated with a napkin on their lap for so long.

Midlife men have candidly shared they are afraid

they will lose their libido. Some have already experienced it slipping. They have lived with continual sexual thoughts for so long, they've allowed it to define themselves and their masculinity. Without ongoing sexual images, they feel less virile. They seem to be so happy to have sexual thoughts and reactions, they can't help themselves from sharing them with us!

Does this forgive men who express their sexual desires inappropriately? Does it suggest grace for those who press for sex too early. No. However, it does explain why some men behave the way they do. They aren't socially savvy enough to realize how off-putting it is. Perhaps they've been schooled by porno flicks to believe that women like this. After all, the men in the videos always seem to get the hot babe, right?

So while I'm not saying to accept inappropriate sexual talk or behavior from anyone, those with mid to higher levels of testosterone seem to have sex on their mind more often than those with lower levels. And women with higher testosterone levels can behave similarly to men with high levels, too.

What's your take on how testosterone can inadvertently run some behaviors? How do you manage it if you have a higher level, or if someone you're dating has a higher level and is always expressing their sexual interest to you

Beyond face value

In midlife dating, we repeatedly hear, "Don't judge a book by it's cover." At this point in our lives most of us have wrinkles, sags and perhaps even some scars or skin discolerations. Yet it takes a lot, usually, to look beyond the surface image.

So what do you do when someone has a facial feature that absorbs much of your attention? How do you see the person who lies beneath?

I recently had the opportunity to share a small-group dinner table conversation with a man who deals with this every day.

Ngahi Bidois is a New Zealand Maori motivational speaker. His face is mostly covered with an intricate traditional Maori tattoo called ta moko.

His face is mostly covered with a tattoo.

At first, I found myself stealing glances not wanting to stare. But in a small group, I could look closely at the pattern while he conversed with others. However, I noticed how quickly my fascination with his facial tattoo waned and soon I began to focus on his expressive and soft brown eyes and engaging smile. His spirit, heart, humor and intelligence emerged delightfully. In no time, I found I didn't even notice the inked design.

In "Yummy is as yummy does" I talk about how a man's attractiveness increases as his kindness, thoughtfulness, humor and caring emerge. He may not be traditionally handsome, but becomes yummier as a special personality is revealed. Yet, most of us don't have to put this concept to the test as frequently as Ngahi does.

Sometimes I can remember to look beyond the surface, but I admit I also fall prey to deleting online profiles of men who sound good when reading their description, but their pictures aren't "my type." It's a common complaint that daters don't give others a chance if they don't look appealing. It's also a common fear that when you meet someone for that first coffee encounter, they will turn on their heel without even saying hello once they see you.

Ngahi is a great reminder of how we can miss out on a treasure if we make too-quick decisions based on only surface signs. By the end of dinner, I was marveling at how handsome he was. (He's married, so not a potential date, but the lesson is still a good one.)

Dating in the time of narcissism

I like to think of myself as a generally positive person, but I have my pet peeves. Self-absorption is one of them, although I'm guessing I can act in ways that seem self-centered to others.

Over the last few years, I've noticed others acting in ways that seem narcissistic. The visitors to the church next to my house who park extending two feet into my driveway. The woman at exercise class who put her bag on top of mine along the wall, meaning I would have to move it when I needed to get my weights out, when there was plenty of other space available for her to put her bag.

In the dating world this self-focus can be glaring.

However, it's in the dating world that this self-focus can be glaring. In the span of a week, two men who have shown interest in me have committed what I consider egregious acts of selfish behaviors.

Last week I hosted a small pot luck dinner party. Potential suitor #1 called a few days before to RSVP and asked what he could bring that didn't require cooking, since he doesn't cook. I suggested he bring a few bottles of wine, explaining no one else had volunteered that. He thought that was a superb idea and said he'd see me two days hence.

The appointed gathering time came and went. The other guests arrived with their contribution One brought a bottle of wine. After waiting an hour, we decided to eat without Suitor #1. I checked my cell phone numerous times thinking he would call to explain his absence. He never did. Not that evening, the next day, nor yet.

I scratch my head wondering how could someone who knew they had a key component to a small collaborative dinner party fail to arrive, and then to not even call to explain himself. Might he have had some emergency? I am tempted to call, but think he would have reached out if this were so. If/when he ever does call, I have my first words ready: "I'm glad you're out of the coma, as that's the only acceptable ex-

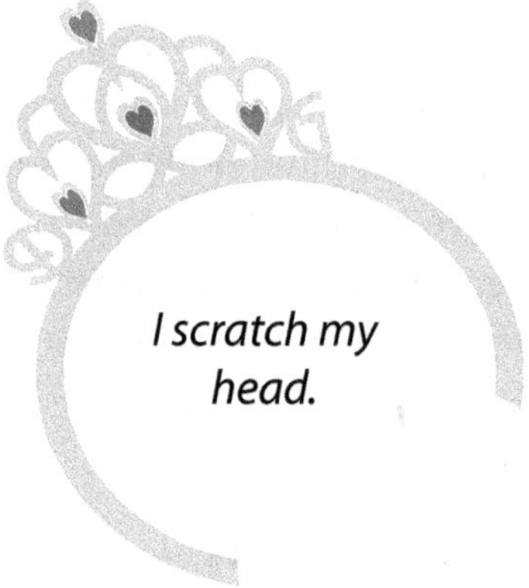

planation for your not showing up for a small soiree to which you knew you were bringing a key component." I doubt he'll call back after that.

Today, another example occurred. Potential Suitor #2 and I have met several times and speak regularly even though we live 1000 miles apart. He's flown to visit me a few times.

On an upcoming trip, I was going to be changing planes in his city, so before I booked the ticket I called and asked if he wanted to rendezvous and if so, I'd arrange for a very early flight into his city, and a later-than-needed flight to my destination. He thought that was great, telling me he knew the perfect restaurant where we could linger for hours and enjoy each other's company.

I sent him my itinerary with flight information.

I texted him when my flight landed telling him I'd arrived. Nothing back. I called when I exited the secure area. Voice mail. I texted again; nothing. Called again. Voice mail. I waited 30 minutes and tried again. I decided he forgot or changed his plans and forgot to tell me. I entered the long security line and headed toward the gates. I had 4.5 hours to kill.

Two hours after our appointed meeting time he called. He had forgotten. He apologized profusely and said he'd be right out to the airport, a 30-minute drive. I said I was very upset, as I'd gotten up at 4:00 to take the earlier flight when I could have taken a later one. I'd been waiting for him for 2 hours. He shouldn't bother coming as I wasn't in the mood. He said he understood why I was upset and apologized again. We hung up.

We all make mistakes. We forget. We're not as organized as we should be and something slips. I'm willing to forgive if it happens once in a blue moon, but only if the person has some deposits in their Bank of Grace. Both these men had made promises in the past they hadn't kept. Usually that's enough for me to cut ties. They are both intelligent, articulate, fun, and good conversationalists. I gave them grace in the past. But these transgressions are the nails in the coffin.

We all know that someone's behavior screams the kind of person they are. Yet if we like them, we allow them grace, which can be kind. However, if their self-absorption happens way too often, no matter how interesting they are, we have to respect ourselves enough to not let their less-than-thoughtful behavior stand. We have to cut the ties or they will continue, as it's doubtful their behavior will change.

Sex talk too soon

A new man started pursuing me and after a few calls shared how much he liked me. I had made no sexual innuendos nor teasing, so was taken aback when he said, "I want to make love to you." I've heard this from a number of men and generally shake it off as they are lonely and horny and socially awkward reentering the dating world so don't realize how off-putting that can be.

I've had others tell me before, during or immediately after a first date what they fantasize our doing together — and I don't mean going to the movies! They have concocted their own movie of us in their head, one that would receive an x rating!

I gave the new man the benefit of a doubt and agreed to dinner as he had other positive attributes. He behaved himself throughout and didn't get grabby during the parting hug.

However the next day he called to tell me how attracted he was to me, how he had trouble sleeping because he kept thinking of me, then recounting in detail his erotic dream of us. Too much information!

I've become flummoxed at this too-much-sex-talk-too-soon approach, but am wondering if I'm just naive. Does this really work to bed women? Are a sufficient number of women horny enough to say, "Hey baby, let's make your dream a reality!"? Do women really find this kind of down-and-dirty talk appealing when they barely know the guy?

Are they so hungry for sex that they don't know they're repelling women?

These men are successful, educated, articulate 50- and 60-year-olds. Are they so hungry for sex that they don't know they are repelling the women they intend to attract? Or do they intend to attract women who are quick to jump in bed with anyone who invites them? Has midlife dating become filled with dirty old men?

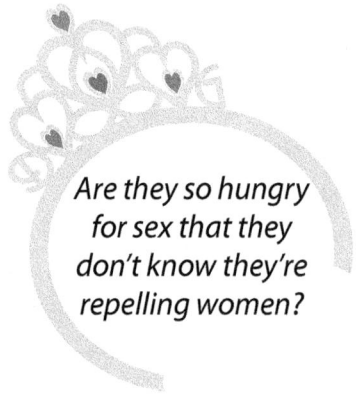

Are there really only a few of us who appreciate a gentleman who treats us like a lady? I am not a prude — there is a time and place for randy talk — but before, during or right after a first date isn't it for me. Perhaps I'm out of step with wanting to actually have a close connection with someone first.

I asked a savvy, intelligent gentleman about this and he said, "Successful guys are now aware that they are in high demand. They are being very blunt about what they want. And the fact is that real ladies are diminishing and fast chicks are multiplying. You are losing the battle. Most guys don't know how to speak to a lady and society/technology is only making it worse."

Sigh.

Another successful, educated business exec/lawyer and I have been communicating for a month because he's currently on a long business trip. We haven't been overtly flirting, just talking by IM, not even voice. Yesterday, he sent me a naked pic of himself, unsolicited. I didn't know quite how to respond, so just said "thanks." He wrote back an irate email saying I was hiding because I didn't send back naked pics of myself.

A-huh.

It seems the hunt for gentlemen is like trying to find white tigers. We know they're out there, but we have to keep weeding out the common ones.

What's your opinion about sexually explicit talk before, during or immediately after a first date? How have you responded when someone goes "there" too soon?

Are you trying to date men who think they are hotter than they are?

He's got a comb over, beer belly, and has donned a wrinkled shirt. Yet he thinks he's James Bond. George Clooney. God's gift to women.

Why?

Because he gets a lot of attention from ladies. Especially over-40 single women.

Why?

Because there are more midlife single women than men over 40. Women in that age group have learned to go after what they want. And they want a man. Even the men described above.

Why?

These women have held out for the man of their dreams and been disappointed that the one(s) they thought was close, turned out to be a cheater, a ne'er-do-well, or emotionally unavailable. So they've lowered their expectations. Now they just want a man who will treat them nicely.

Average-looking single men have recounted how women throw themselves at them. The women make overt sexual advances on the first date. The men are inundated with women inviting them over for dinner and a little something-something for dessert. The man feels he's got mojo oozing out his pores.

Author Bernard Salt calls this "hotness delusion syndrome." While women can suffer from it as well, it seems particularly pronounced in middle-aged men who've stuck their toe — or more — in the dating pool. They feel they are not only in the candy shop, but immersed in a vat of delicious morsels — they can't wait to try the next one. There's an unending supply to quench their desires.

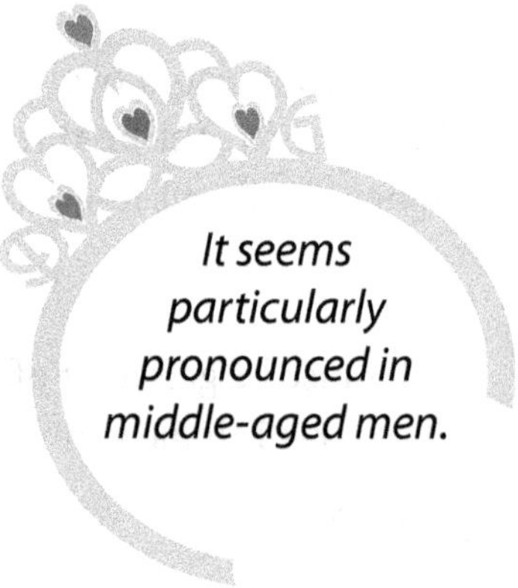
It seems particularly pronounced in middle-aged men.

So what to do when you encounter one of these delusional ones? Generally, I'd say run in the other direction. It's unlikely he's going to be ready for the reality of the work and compromise a real relationship takes. If the relationship takes any tweaking (as relationships do), he's gone as he can always get someone new in a flash.

However, if you feel you want to stick it out, you'll have to feed that delusion and reinforce his perceived hotness. If you tell him the truth — that his ear hairs need trimmed, or he needs to lose 30 pounds, or he should buy iron-free shirts — he'll be dejected and you'll be rejected.

So if he's self-aware enough to know that his hotness is unusual and unexpected, he's a keeper. As long as he doesn't begin to believe that he should only be dating Jennifer Aniston.

How much is too much initiative in dating?

Karen writes: "I am afraid I am too assertive. I start taking the lead when the man won't or doesn't. I see simple solutions (where and when to meet) and make suggestions. Is this really a bad thing?"

DG responds: If you are a dominatrix, you have stuck gold by finding many submissive men!

Not that there's anything wrong with that if that's what your into. I have now learned that "goddess" is a very popular term in the dom/sub world — but unfortunately that's not what floats my boat. But I've had many, many men assume this is the case and have eagerly sought me out — but not too eagerly as that would mean they weren't a sub!

But it doesn't sound like that's what you want. I have experienced your situation as well. If you want an assertive man, not a passive one, then yes, your initiating will be a problem. I found in my marriage I did 95% of the initiating of anything and it got tiresome.

So now in dating, when a man flirts, he has to initiate: "Shall we get together." To which I've learned to respond, "I'd like that very much." If he does nothing from that, I know he's not that interested. If he says, "Great. Shall we have lunch or coffee?" I say, "I'd prefer coffee." He has to suggest dates, times, places. I don't want to sound evasive — in fact I want to sound encouraging! If I have to initiate closing the deal, I know he's not very demonstrative (and I need a strong man or I'll run all over him and be frustrated) and I let him go.

Karen: Do I offer to pay/split or not?

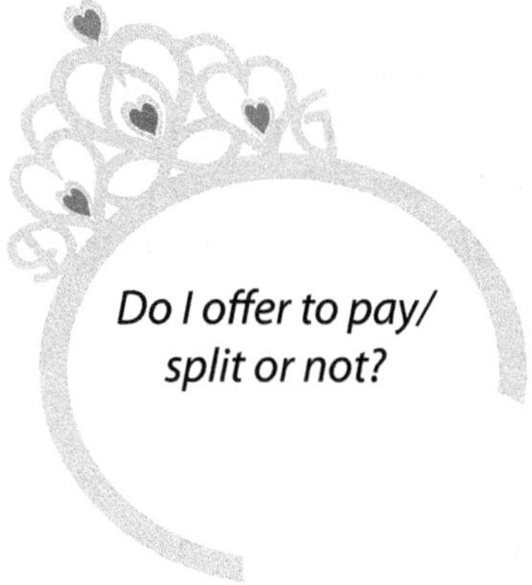
Do I offer to pay/
split or not?

DG: Generally, men like to show they are a good provider, especially midlife men, and they will want to pick up the check, sometimes even if they have no interest in seeing you again.

This is one of the reasons I agree to only coffee for the first date. If we are ordering at the same time (meaning he didn't get there first and order his while waiting for me), I always reach for my wallet. Ninety-five percent of the time, the man will say, "I've got this," to which I smile and say, "Thank you." If he's already ordered, he will typically say, "What can I get you?" He's being the host.

If we'd hit it off really well on the phone and I'm

seduced into lunch with him for the first encounter (NEVER DINNER!!!), when the check comes, I again reach for my wallet. I'll usually say, "How would you like to handle this?" Nearly all the time he'll say, "I've got it." If he says, "Let's split it" it means he isn't attracted to you. No problem. Pay up and be on your way. Don't look for a kiss goodbye!

I've learned men like — really like — that you offered, but didn't insist on splitting it.

They feel emasculated if you insist when they've offered to treat. They get a little thrill out of treating; it makes them feel more manly. Don't steal that from them by insisting on splitting the check.

After you've gone out a few times, then you can offer to take him to your favorite place, cook for him, pack a picnic, etc.

(Warning: I've learned many men interpret an invitation to your house as really an invitation for sex. One man showed up with his shaving kit on our second date when I'd invited him for dinner! If you're not ready for that to happen, don't invite him to your house — even for lunch! Or make sure there's another couple and they agree to not leave until he has. Maybe I've just had too many who make this assumption, but now I don't invite men to my house for a while. And there are definitely no sleepovers until I've visited his home at least once.)

Karen: Do I offer to drive to where he is or meet 1/2 way? I often date outside my small town.

DG: If he's interested, he'll offer to make the drive to you. However, he may accept your offer to meet him half way. Don't offer to drive to his city/town. If he says, "Let me know when you're in my town" he has no interest in you, unless he has no car.

Men like to take care of women and doing the bulk of the driving is one way of doing that. However, if you're an hour away he will appreciate your even offering to split the driving chore. On subsequent dates, you may offer to take turns, but let him drive to you (or meet half way) for the first few encounters.

Karen: I really have a problem with not sharing the burden of dating. I'll work on it.

When you realize men perceive this as taking something away from them, it gets easier to accept their overtures. They like to "win you over" and woo you. Let them!

Dance card unfilled

At my professional association conference last week I got a lot of attention. I was very visible in a number of sessions, so had a lot of people acknowledge my contributions. In one session, I made a joke about looking for dance partners for the gala.

About a dozen men came up to me afterward saying they wanted a slot on my dance card. I smiled and agreed.

I moseyed into the ballroom after the DJ began and looked for my pre-determined dance partners. One grabbed me and escorted me to the floor. We had a fun couple of dances. I noticed others stationed near the floor's edge.

Another spun me for a few songs. Turns out — unbeknownst to me — that he'd been on his country's Dancing with the Stars! No wonder he was a good dancer!

But that was it. Many of the others who had requested dances didn't make it into the ballroom — obviously something else distracted them. But I'm curious about those who were close enough to the dance floor to see that I was available. Were they just being nice to ask beforehand for a dance?

It makes me ponder — once again — about curious male behavior. I know women tend to over think things like this, but it's indicative of so much about dating. Men show interest then don't follow through.

Conceivably these guys got involved with others with whom they were chatting, or maybe they thought I was otherwise engaged with those who'd taken me to the dance floor. Or maybe they didn't like the way I danced! Who knows?

Of course, I could have reminded them they were on my dance card, but that felt a bit desperate. If I was really hankering for a dance, I could have done that. But I don't relish hunting down men who've shown interest but don't deliver.

I wanted to share this story for other women who end up scratching their heads wondering why men show interest, then disappear. Bottom line: Don't take it personally. They got distracted by something and so don't wait for them to come around. Just keep dancing.

Resources

Make sure to download your free eBook Attract Your Next Great Mate: Dating Advice From Top Relationship Experts *at www. DatingGoddess.com/freebie*

Afterword

At the time of this writing, I have not yet found my true King Charming. I continue my search with verve. I've become more discerning about what I want and don't want. I've met some wonderful men pals — my treasures — who continue to be in touch.

I wish you much luck in your adventure. It will be fun and frustrating, exhilarating and exasperating, and sexy or sexless. So much depends on you, your approach and your attitude. My books are designed to help you enjoy as much as possible and ward off unpleasantness. But nearly all adventures have wonderful highs as well as a few lows. If you know that going in and arm yourself with information on what to expect, you'll have more of the positives and fewer of the negatives.

Please drop by www.DatingGoddess.com and join in the discussion and report on your experiences.

Dating Goddess

Resources

Go to www.datinggoddess.com to access a variety of useful resources. We work to suggest resources we think have value.

Dating and relationship book reviews

These reviews will save you time and money as I've given you my take on specific books, CDs and more. Some are worth your effort to buy and read or listen to them — some are not. We're always adding new book reviews, so check frequently. We'll also notify our mailing list when new resources are added.

Dating site links

There are a lot of dating sites on the Internet. I've listed the ones I think are worth investigating.

Dating products and tools

Dating can be daunting. We're continually looking at

ways to make it easier and more fun. We'll provide info on games, tools, even date-wear that will help others know you're available, or help you get to know potential suitors better.

Dating and relationship advice sites

Advice "experts" abound on the Internet as anyone can self-proclaim themseves as expert — even if they haven't dated in 30 years and never in midlife. I've worked to find experts who's advice I generally think is solid.

Midlife recources

We'll feature Web sites, books, events and other resources we think might interest you.

Newly discovered resources

I'll add other resources as we discover them, subscribe to our mailing list to get the scoop as soon as we find them. Go to www.DatingGoddess.com to register for our mailing list. Don't worry, we won't sell or give your email to anyone.

Acknowledgments

Let me start by acknowledging the 112 men who helped trigger the lessons contained in this book. Some prompted several! They remain nameless here to protect their identity, although most would recognize references to them. Plus the thousands more whose winks, emails and calls didn't result in a date, but helped me learn the dating game. And all those men who I emailed who never responded — such a blessing to have them weed themselves out.

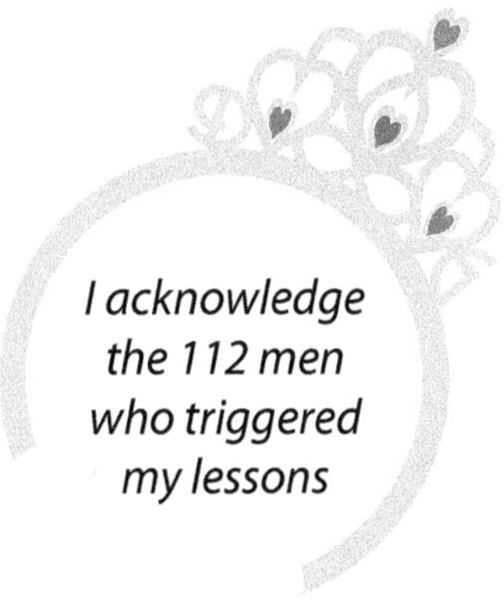
I acknowledge the 112 men who triggered my lessons

I'd like to thank my Seven Sisters mastermind group for the tremendous brainstorming, noodling, strategizing and encouragement. I wouldn't have begun this project without the prodding of Val Cade, Chris Clarke-Epstein, Mariah Burton Nelson, Sue Dyer, Sam Horn and Marilynn Mobley.

Thank you to my good friends who've listened to my dating stories ad nauseam, and whose support and wisdom are embedded in this text. Ed Betts, Ken Braly, Bruce Daley, Tom Drews, Elaine Floyd, Paulette Ensign, Scott Friedman, Craig Harrison, Mary Jansen, Tom Johnson, Sandy Jones, Mary Kilkenny, Ellie Klevins, Patrick Lynch, Mary Marcdante, Barbara McNichol, Ann Peterson, Anthony Ramsey, Caterina Rando, Kristy Rogers, Jana Stanfield, Holly Steil, Terry Tepliz, and George Walther, thank you.

The Adventures in Delicious Dating After 40 series

The Adventures in Delicious Dating After 40 series is designed to help you understand your own midlife dating journey. It is not a road map, as we all take different routes. It is a guide to help you understand yourself, midlife men, and the dating process. Hopefully, you'll not only learn from the lessons and insights shared in this series, but you'll examine how they apply — or don't — to your own dating adventure.

You'll get the scoop on what you need to know, what's changed since you last dated, and how to navigate inevitable bumps in the road.

Following is an overview of each book in the series and a sampling of some of the chapter titles. All are detailed at www.DatingGoddess.com.

Date or Wait: Are You Ready for Mr. Great?

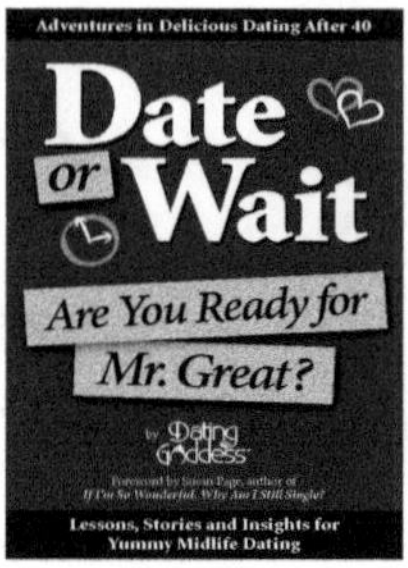
Adventures in Delicious Dating After 40
Date
or
Wait
Are You Ready for
Mr. Great?
by Dating Goddess
Lessons, Stories and Insights for
Yummy Midlife Dating

Are you ready for a special man in your life? You have a great life. But you know you'd like a special man to share it. You think you're ready to date, but you haven't done it in a while.

What should you consider before you actually start dating full bore? Even if you've reentered the dating world, this will give you a foundation of attitude and philosophy to make your adventure more fulfilling.

Sample chapters

- From hurt to flirt
- Dating is like Baskin-Robbins
- You've got to kiss a lot of…princes!
- What's your definition of dating success?
- Are you open to receiving?
- Dating: A self-designed personal-growth workshop
- Hands-on dating research
- Being present to the presents
- Being aggressively single
- Approaching dating like a buffet
- Is Brad Pitt ruining your love life?
- Treasures can come in dented packages

Assessing Your Assets: Why You're A Great Catch

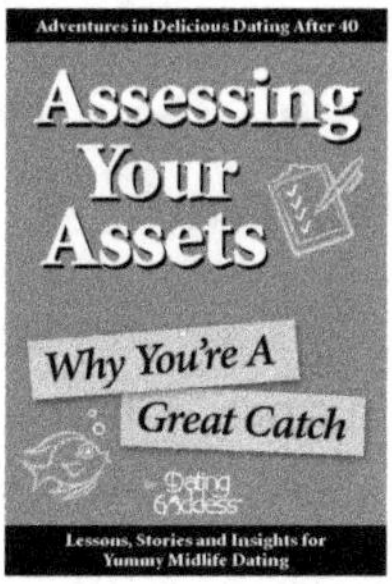

You have many wonderful qualities. But it's easy to focus on one's flaws — at least what seem like flaws to you. However, to the right man your imperfections are endearing, attractive and lovable. You have to be clear what you offer a man who will find you enchanting.

Assessing Your Assets helps you look at what you bring to a new relationship. It will help you see your good points so you'll approach dating with more confidence.

Sample chapters

- Don't think you are damaged goods
- You are (probably) more attractive than you think!
- They aren't called "hate handles"
- Are you a good man picker?
- What are your deal breakers?
- Are you arguing your limitations?
- Turn your liabilities into assets
- The strong vs. nice woman debate
- Is your sense of humor stunting your dating?
- Why are we drawn to bad boys?
- The zest test

In Search of King Charming: Who Do I Want to Share My Throne?

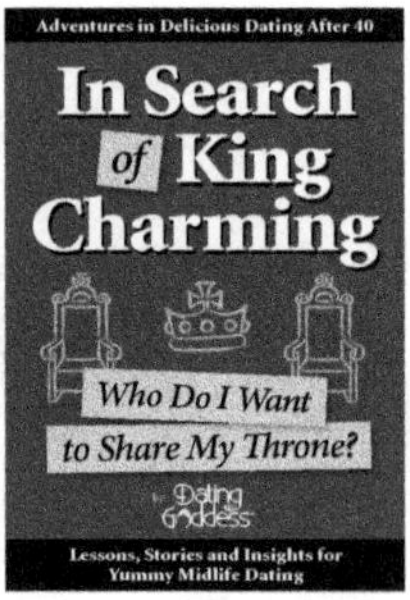

You are no longer looking for "Prince" Charming because you are a queen. You want someone who is at your level, not groveling at your feet. You want a king — someone who's your equal and with whom you can rule the throne together!

This book focuses on helping you better define what you want beyond tall, dark and handsome! You'll consider characteristics you might not have thought of before. You'll look at what you want now.

Sample chapters

- Building your Franken-boyfriend
- What's your "perfect boyfriend's" job description?
- A man to go with your wardrobe
- In search of the elusive good kisser
- When you're clear on what you want, it appears
- Are you dating the same guy in different bodies?
- Does he fit in your world?
- What's your kissing quotient?
- Is your guy's loving muscle strong?
- Do you both have the same dating rhythm?

Embracing Midlife Men: Insights Into Curious Behaviors

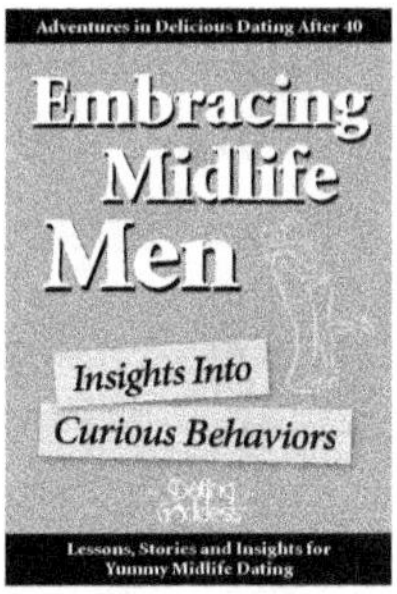

Do you sometimes scratch your head after interacting with a midlife man, wondering, "What could he possibly be thinking?" Especially if it's before, during or after a date with a man who presumably wants to impress you!

This book focuses on better understanding midlife men's behaviors. When you grasp what's going on in his head it's much easier to embrace him. Men are wondrous creatures, so we need to understand them better and love them for who they are.

Sample chapters

- Men are like shoes
- Why men disappear when it gets serious
- Chivalry isn't dead—but it seems to be hibernating
- Do men want feisty women?
- Midlife men have forgotten how to date
- Are you getting prime time from your man?
- When a man tells you what he paid for things
- Does he treat you like his ex?
- Has Greg Behrendt done women a disservice?
- Tales of woo

Dipping Your Toe in the Dating Pool: Dive In Without Belly Flopping

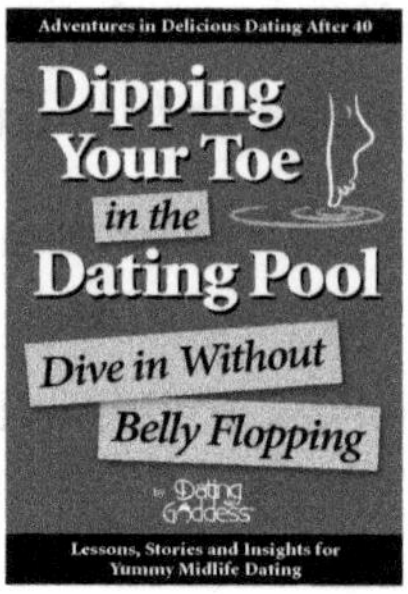

You've decided you are ready — you want to start dating. Maybe you've already had a few coffee dates with several men. You want to be as successful as possible on your dating adventure.

This book focuses on getting started on your dating adventures. We cover what you need to know as you begin your journey.

Sample chapters

- Do you have the right datewear?
- Dating with integrity
- Building your rejection muscle
- When "be yourself" is questionable advice
- Faux beaus and practice dating
- Are you making bad decisions out of loneliness?
- Being "in wonder" about your date's behavior
- When do you feel most vulnerable in dating?
- Are you out of his league — or he yours?
- Why listening is so seductive

Winning at the Online Dating Game: Stack the Deck in Your Favor

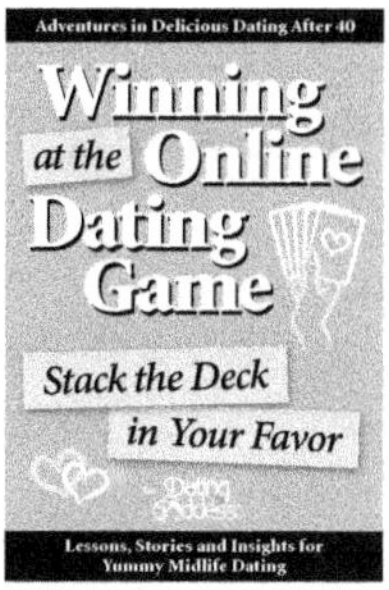

Internet dating can be frustrating or fruitful. It will be much less exasperating if you know how to read and weed out men's profiles that aren't appropriate for you. And you'll have a steady stream of potential suitors if you know how to write a compelling profile for yourself.

This book focuses on the ins and outs of online dating. How to play the game, which has it's own rules and language. If you don't understand how online dating works, you'll waste a lot of time connecting with men who are not a possible fit for you.

Sample chapters

- Shopping for men
- Safe online dating
- Is 21st Century dating unnatural?
- What do men look at in your profile?
- Euphemisms uncovered
- Are you describing yourself compellingly?
- No, I will not be dating your Harley
- Playing the online dating game
- Scantily clothed pictures

Check Him Out Before Going Out: Avoiding Dud Dates

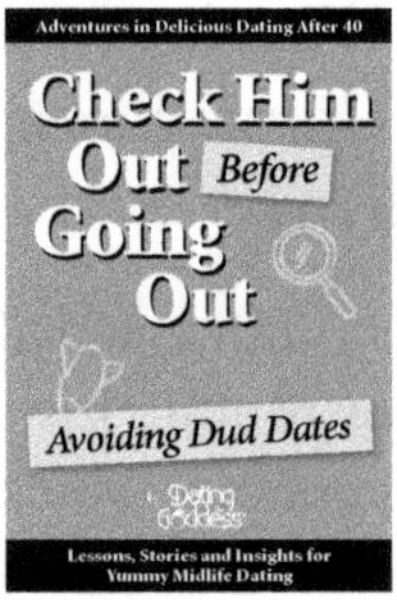

Under the cloak of the anonymity that email and the phone provides, men often reveal more than they intend. If you ask the right questions you can find out a lot about his values and view of the world after just an interaction or two.

This book focuses on what you need to ask before agreeing to even a coffee date. You need to vet the men who email and call you to ensure you're not likely to waste your time with men who clearly aren't a match.

Sample chapters

- Becoming smitten with the fantasy
- Can Google help — or hinder — your dating life?
- Qualify your potential dates before meeting
- The art of consideration
- Anticipating a big date is like awaiting Santa
- Being seduced by what he is over who he is
- Are you his spare?
- My boyfriend, whom I haven't met
- When canceling is the right thing to do
- Politics, religion and sex — oh my!

First-Rate First Dates: Increasing the Chances of a Second Date

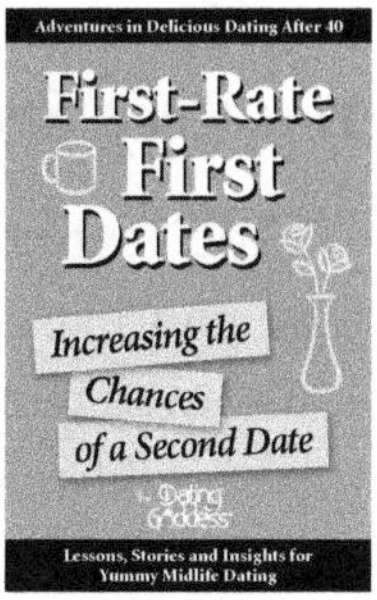

You can tell a lot about someone within the first 30 minutes. What does he talk about? Does he ask you questions? If so, what does he want to know about you? What do you need to know about him? How does he treat you? How does he treat those around you?

This book focuses on what goes on during the first date. How do you determine if you want a second date? What you can do to increase the likelihood your date will ask you for a second? That is if you want a repeat!

Sample chapters

- Start with coffee
- How do you greet him?
- When it clicks, throw out some of your criteria
- Tracking your date's score
- Clues a guy is just looking for a booty call
- 12 signs he won't be asking for a second date
- First-date red flags that this guy isn't for you
- Honesty is not always the best policy
- Chemistry, or does he make my toes curl?
- Women's first-date blunders

Real Deal or Faux Beau: Should You Keep Seeing Him?

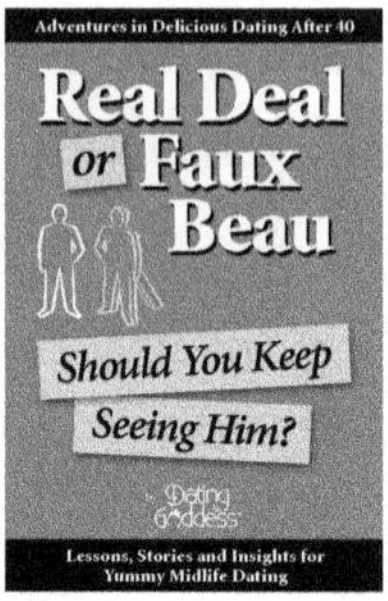

You've begun to go out with a man you like. How do you decide if you should continue seeing him, or if you should release him because he's not The One?

This book focuses on second dates and beyond. During the dating process you are both assessing if you want to keep seeing each other. This book helps you determine what questions you need to ask yourself.

Sample chapters

- Deciding to see him again or not
- What's your date's Delight/Disappointment Scale score?
- Broaching tough conversations
- "I want to respect me in the morning"
- Does he invite you to his place?
- Are you stingy in dating?
- When his hand is on your knee too soon
- Easy way to ask hard questions
- Rose-colored glasses obscure red flags
- If his stories don't add up, subtract yourself

Multidating Responsibly: Play the Field Without Being A Player

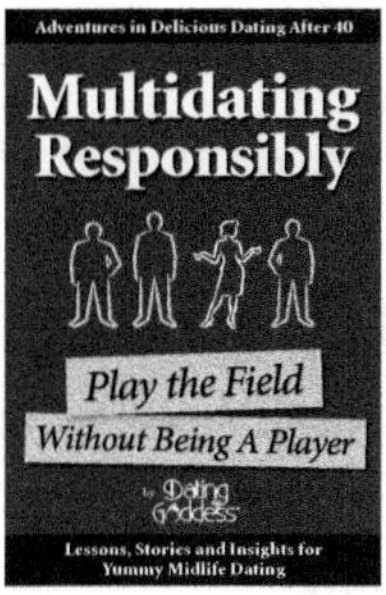

Playing the field is frowned on in some circles. There are definitely appropriate and inappropriate ways to date several men simultaneously.

This book focuses on how to date around responsibly and with integrity without leading men on. If you do it with honesty, you can date several people at once until you're both ready to focus only on each other.

Sample chapters

- "Pimpin'" — Dating multiple guys
- Multi-dating pros and cons
- Your Date-A-Base — tracking multiple suitors
- "Hot bunking" your beaus
- Are you a "Let's Make a Deal" type of dater?
- Assume there are other women
- Dating's revolving door
- How long do you hedge your bet?
- Beware of multi-tasking when multi-dating
- Back burner beaus
- The boyfriend phone

Moving On Gracefully: Break Up Without Heartache

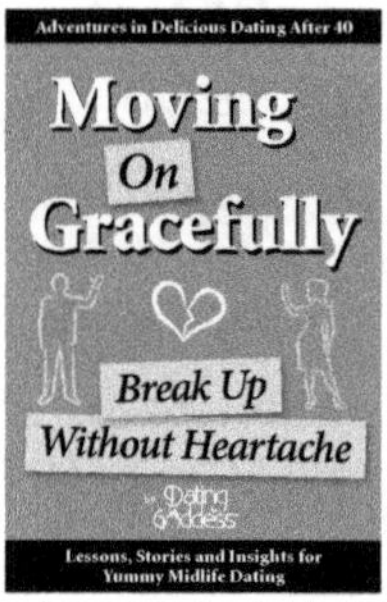

"Breaking up" sounds so high school, doesn't it? But part of the dating process is saying something when one of you decides not to date the other anymore. Going "poof" is not a mature or respectful option in midlife.

This book focuses on surviving a breakup, whether you initiate it or not. Either way, it's never easy to break up if you have developed any fondness toward the other.

Sample chapters

- Hello — goodbye: How to say no thanks after meeting
- Releasing back into the dating pool
- 50 ways to leave your lover? 4 ways not to leave your suitor
- Breaking up is hard to do — right
- Why men go "poof"
- How to trump being dumped
- When breaking up is a "Get Out of Jail Free" card
- How to detect the end is near
- Failed relationships' blessings
- He's broken up with you — he just didn't tell you
- Rejection is protection

From Fear to Frolic: Get Naked Without Getting Embarrassed

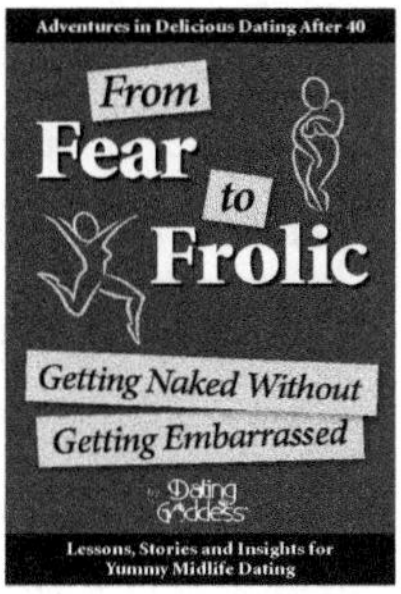

This book focuses on what you need to consider and know before getting physically intimate with a man you're dating. This is nerve-wracking to many midlife women. This book will prepare you.

Sample chapters

- Sleepover do's and don'ts
- Does he want in your life — or just in your bedroom?
- Getting naked with him the first time
- An excuse to seduce or how important is bed-room bliss?
- What to ask yourself before getting naked with him
- Are you and your guy on the same sexual time line?
- Sharing your sexual owner's manual with him
- What women need from a man before having sex
- Why too-soon midlife sex is like non-fat food
- How dating sex is like waffles
- Too-soon seduction: "I'm special, but not THAT special"

Ironing Out Dating Wrinkles: Work Through Challenges Without Getting Steamed

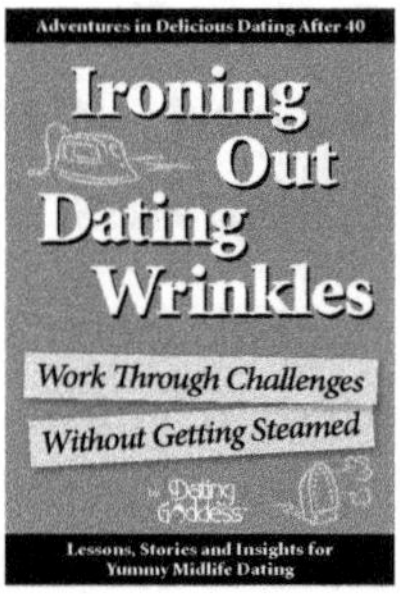

Nearly all relationships have some ups and downs. Part of getting to know someone is knowing how they work through relationship misunderstandings.

This book focuses on how to work through the inevitable hiccups that happen when you are getting to know each other. If you can both deal with challenges, the bond deepens and you find yourself smitten.

Sample chapters

- When your guy vexes you, ask what your highest self would do
- The first fight
- You want boo; he wants boo-ty
- Where's the line between getting your needs met and being selfish?
- Expressing your upset with your guy
- Is his toothbrush in your cabinet too soon?
- Do you love how he loves you?
- Is he collecting data on how to make you happy?
- Be careful of being smitten
- Exclusivity: How and when to broach it